The Soul of Counseling

Publisher's Note

This publication is designed to provide accurate and authoritative information in regard to the subject matter covered. It is sold with the understanding that the publisher is not engaged in rendering psychological, medical, or other professional service.

Books in The Practical Therapist Series® present authoritative answers to the question, "What-do-I-do-now-and-how-do-I-do-it?" in the practice of psychotherapy, bringing the wisdom and experience of expert mentors to the practicing therapist. A book, however, is no substitute for thorough professional training and adherence to ethical and legal standards. At minimum:

- *The practitioner must be qualified to practice psychotherapy.*
- *Clients participate in psychotherapy only with informed consent.*
- *The practitioner must not "guarantee" a specific outcome.*

— Robert E. Alberti, Ph.D., Publisher

The Soul of Counseling

A New Model for Understanding Human Experience

Dwight Webb, Ph.D.

The Practical Therapist Series®

Impact Publishers®
ATASCADERO, CALIFORNIA

ATTENTION ORGANIZATIONS AND CORPORATIONS:
This book is available at quantity discounts on bulk purchases for educational, business, or sales promotional use. For further information, please contact Impact Publishers, P.O. Box 6016, Atascadero, California 93423-6016. Phone 805-466-5917, e-mail: info@impactpublishers.com

Library of Congress Cataloging-in-Publication Data

Webb, Dwight, 1933-
    The soul of counseling : a new model for understanding human experience / Dwight Webb.
        p. cm.
    Includes bibliographical references and index.
    ISBN 1-886230-59-5 (alk. paper)
        1. Counseling—Religious aspects. 2. Psychology and religion.
        3. Spirituality—Psychology. I. Title.
BF637.C6W383 2005
206'.1—dc22
                                                                    2004026735

Impact Publishers and colophon are registered trademarks of Impact Publishers, Inc.

Cover design by Sharon Wood Schnare, San Luis Obispo, California
Printed in the United States of America on acid-free paper.
Published by **Impact 🐾 Publishers®**
POST OFFICE BOX 6016
ATASCADERO, CALIFORNIA 93423-6016
www.impactpublishers.com

Dedication

To my mentor, **William R. (Cherry) Parker**. *This man was whole, balanced, joyful, wise, humorous, and knowledgeable. He loved life, loved people, loved learning and loved to laugh. His spirit was like a magnet. Students were drawn to his enthusiasm, his wit and wisdom, in short, his soul. He was a psychologist, a professor, and the founder and director of the Speech and Hearing Clinic at the University of Redlands. And most of all, he was a splendid human being! I dedicate this book to him with the following eulogy.*

The Gift of a Lifetime

Cherry knew that love was at the center of everything.
He taught it, and lived it.
Giving and receiving love was like breathing to him

His humor and laughter warmed us all,
Revealing a heart so generous and exuding such a vitality
That we couldn't help but love life more because of him

His spirit would not be contained,
Flowing richly and freely to all
Who would encounter him

He cut through all that was pretense
With the grace of his wit, and intuitive morality of his soul

Hope and optimism were among the gifts he gave us
Always encouraging and reminding us of our power within
The power of becoming more fully human

My life was transformed by this man
And all who I have touched are the beneficiaries

Truly a radiant being, we carry his legacy of love
Passing on the torch of his life

— *Dwight Webb*

Contents

Permissions

Competencies for Integrating Spirituality into Counseling used with permission of ASERVIC (Association for Spiritual, Ethical, and Religious Values in Counseling), a division of The American Counseling Association. www.ASERVIC.com.

Poem "If I Can Stop One Heart from Breaking" by Emily Dickinson reprinted by permission of the publishers and the Trustees of Amherst College from the *Poems Of Emily Dickinson*, Thomas H. Johnson, ed., Cambridge, MA: The Belknap Press of Harvard University Press, Copyright 1951, 1955, 1979 by the President and Fellows of Harvard College.

Excerpt from *The Prophet* by Kahlil Gibran used by permission of Alfred A. Knopf, a division of Random House, Inc. Copyright 1923 and renewed by Administrators C.T.A. of Kahlil Gibran Estate and Mary G. Gibran.

"All Kinds of Weather Friends" by Susan Joy, copyright 1973, 1978, 2004. Used with permission, all rights reserved, Amherst NH: BMI (Boston Post Road).

"Holy Now" by Peter Mayer used with permission from his album, *Million Mile Minds*, 2001. Available by email at peppermint@actwin.com.

Excerpts from *Integrating Spirituality into Treatment: Resources for Practitioners*, W. R. Miller and C. E. Thoresen, copyright 1999, reprinted with permission of the American Psychological Association. Washington.

Excerpts from *A Way of Being* by Carl Rogers, copyright 1980, pages reprinted with permission of Houghton Mifflin Company. All rights reserved.

"Beginning to Be" by Václev Havel is from *Letters to Olga* (Paul Wilson, translator), 1983. New York: Henry Holt and Co., Inc. (The office of the President of the Czech Republic was contacted for permission to use the poem on page 150, and had no record of it. The poem has been widely quoted — usually without reference to the original source in Havel's work.)

Acknowledgements

Thanks to:

- My wife Leslie for her soul support, and for encouraging me to get up from my desk and take walks with her, and for sending our seven-year-old daughter Julia running in to tell me it's time to eat.

- Liam McCarthy of the Personal Counseling Institute in Dublin, Ireland for the invitation and encouragement to present my first paper on spirituality.

- Bob Alberti for believing in this book and for excellent suggestions in shaping my ideas.

- Hugh Hayden, Lorrie Webb Grillo, Angelo Boy, Will Williams, Karen Bouvier, Ginny Holder, and Dick Riedman for early reads and encouraging words.

- Jerry and Marianne Corey, and David Webb for suggestions along the way.

- Laurrie Melizia for putting my rough draft on the computer.

- Nancy Puglisi for her enlightened approach to wholistic health and the courage to offer university courses in spirituality.

- The University of New Hampshire for granting my sabbatical so I could draft this book.

- Michele Thomas, a past president of the Association of Counselor Educators and Supervisors (ACES) for inviting me to be a coordinator of the Spiritual Interest Network along with Laurrie Johnson and Lora Davidson.

- My Prague pilgrim cohorts on the ACES spiritual conferencing trip to the Czech Republic, and to the ACES program committee for sponsoring my presentations in Anaheim, at the American Counseling Association National Convention in 2003.

- My students both in Ireland and at the University of New Hampshire who heard my message of calling out the spiritual nature of counseling, with special thanks to Lisa Houle, Heidi Malardo, Monica Foley and Holly Greenston for enthusiastic support, and to my internship students: Lea Boivert, Jessica Golden, Emily Gross, Maria Marmarou, Adrienne Miller, Brett Mongeon, and Kelly Warren, for good ideas and encouragement.

- Greg Goodman for a thoughtful read and helpful suggestions.

- The all too-numerous-to-list people who have challenged and awakened my spirit along the pathways of my learning, contributing to the strength of my soul, and helping me to fine tune my values, my beliefs, my attitudes, my ideas and my actions.

- All the writers who are referenced in my book, and all my many other teachers who have gifted me with their wisdom.

- Carol Gay for help with technical editing.

- My parents Verna, and Wayne, who nurtured my soul in early years, and to my brother Loren, and my four sons, David, Michael, John and Chris, who continue to nurture my soul.

- Special thanks to Patricia Arredondo, Jon Carlson and Sam Gladding for their prepublication review of my book and their kind and generous words of support. Such encouragement is a primary substance for nourishing the *soul*, and my gratitude awakens in response.

Introduction
Putting the Psyche Back in Psychology

Only within yourself exists that other reality for which you long. I can give you nothing that has not already its being within you. I can throw open no picture gallery but your own soul. All I can give you is the opportunity, the impulse, the key.

— Hermann Hesse

It has been nearly twenty years since Sara arrived at my office, very tense and depressed, to discuss some behavioral problems her daughter was having in preschool. As she began to tell me about what was happening, it became clear to both of us that we could be of most help to her daughter if she were my client. I had no idea in that first session that in the next few weeks she would be telling me about being sexually abused by her father some thirty years earlier, when she was just four and five years old. She had long-since buried these experiences, and said she had never told another soul about it.

I still have a vision of her sobbing, hiding her shame as she dropped her head into her hands. It was a wake-up call for me. I sat stunned, realizing that this was not just a depressed single mom with concerns about her little girl. Here was a person with a seriously wounded *soul*. Her spirit had not merely been dampened, it had been squashed. This awakening was the beginning of reframing how I conceptualized my work in counseling.

❖❖ *Soul — the Taboo Subject*

Psyche is the Greek word for *soul*; psychology literally means the study of the *soul*. Yet, in all my undergraduate and graduate study in psychology, as well as more than three decades as a university professor, I don't remember hearing the idea of *soul* ever discussed. Even in the larger culture, it seems a taboo subject, except within certain religious traditions. When I reflect on all my clients over the years — with dysfunctional behaviors categorized as depression, anxiety, low self-esteem, adjustment disorder, or by some other formal label — it seems to me more accurate to see these symptoms as in some way expressing a deep hurt or insult to their inner psyche — their *soul*.

When I ask groups of my students if they think they have a *soul*, they all say yes, but they don't know how to talk about it, or really want to. It seems uncomfortable to focus on it. They all agree that they have a spiritual dimension, but they don't want to talk about that either. I find this unspoken cultural taboo very interesting.

Throughout my life I have been interested in how I am impacted by significant relationships and events. For as long as I can remember, I have been aware that something within me can be encouraged and inspired or discouraged and dispirited. In my career as a counselor and counselor educator I see this strand of interest in the human spirit throughout my teaching, research and writing, even though I did not frame these pursuits in spiritual language at the time. It is only more recently that the language of spirituality has become more acceptable in the mainstream of academia and the larger professional culture. In the earlier years of my career, it was not safe to enter into the territory of such ethereal topics that dealt with the *soul* or human spirituality.

For example, my doctoral dissertation examined the affective impact of teacher sensitivity on individual differences among students. As a school counselor, I could see students being hurt by those teachers who used sarcasm and humiliation in their attempts to shape their students' behavior. I could see the effects these toxic encounters had on my students' global sense of *self*. I know now, and can say now, that *affective* impact, is *soul* impact! The insensitivity and negativity of particular teachers was spiritually wounding some students. How could humiliation not have this effect?

❖ *Saving Souls*

To some extent, I suppose, we all enter the fields of human services to save *souls*, including our own. We see the underdogs and the walking wounded and realize it doesn't have to be that way. After more than four decades in the field, I have come to see that counseling must engage our *souls*, if there is going to be any saving. It has also become more clear to me that our hope, our faith, our compassion, and our commitment are among the spiritual qualities that connect us to the *soul* dimensions in relationships.

If the focus of our work as professionals is reduced to dealing simply with the manifestations of behavior, affect and cognition, our understanding will be shallow, fragmented, and compartmentalized. We will miss the full spectrum of our ability to respond to the complex interactive wholeness of our clients — their very real inner lives. We will miss the *soul* connection. I believe that unless we claim the *soul* in counseling there will be nothing of meaningful and lasting significance gained. No method, no technique, no intervention based on the purest form of any theory will mean anything if it is only surface attention and professional conformity to traditional protocol. Relationships will be hollow if they are not grounded at the *soul* level of individual meaning. Where do behaviors such as authenticity and generosity arise if not from our human spirit? What good is it to gain knowledge and fail to recognize our own *soul*?

That there is spiritual hunger in contemporary society there can be no doubt. In our mad rush toward materialism, we have lost sight and touch with the balance and harmony we yearn for. In our Western cultural proclivity toward making more money, buying bigger homes and newer cars, we too often neglect the quality of our relationships. We slide past intimacy and authentic encounters, like ships in the night. We seek status as our way of belonging, and settle for indifference with our neighbors instead of kinship and a sense of community.

Yet, in the viscera of our lives, there is a continuing yearning of our *soul* to make sense of it all. We ask: "Who am I? What is the purpose and meaning of my life? Can I make a difference in the scheme of things? How can I have inner peace for myself in this chaotic world?"

I want to be very clear that I am not talking about "religion" here, rather about our inner life. This book is not about any religion, deity or doctrine, and it is not about any mystical experience. Rather, it emphasizes that all humans are spiritual at the core of their being. I call this spiritual core our *soul*. My wish is to demystify and clarify how it is that our *soul* consciousness is manifest in observable and tangible ways.

The implications for counseling and other human services are profound! Brian Thorne (1998) puts it this way: "As our materialistic and electronic culture embraces a network of communications, where the interior life is sacrificed on the altar of efficiency and to the shallowness of the instant response, so the counselors and psychotherapists must commit themselves to a deeper level of experiencing."

Joseph Campbell believed that people will become open to exploring their personal spirituality beyond religion and gain an awareness that connects us to all of life. Elliot Ingersol (1995) suggests that if Campbell is right, and if "spirituality grows into popular understanding as a construct of human development, counselors may truly be on the 'cutting edge,' helping people to engage in what is no less than a developmental revolution."

Certainly many of our constituents are ready for this deeper level of understanding. We have seen this emerging for more than a decade. Mary Bart (1998) reports: "In a 1992 Gallup Poll, 66 percent of the people surveyed said they would prefer to see a professional counselor with spiritual values and beliefs, and 81 percent said they would want to have their own values and beliefs integrated into the counseling process. And yet, in spite of this, most counselor education programs give cursory attention, at best, to the subject of spirituality."

Counseling psychology may or may not be the discipline with which you identify — people helpers come in a wide variety of sizes, colors, and academic backgrounds. I was drawn to train in counseling psychology because it emphasized the importance of contributing to the development of the whole person. It was a major shift from clinical psychology, which focused more on pathology and abnormal behavior. I believe that all of our allied helping professions are evolving toward an openness to humanistic and existential ideas and practices that consider the deeper concerns of meaning and significance in life experience.

This book is for all who work with our fellow humans as a helper. Let's face it, we're all in this together, regardless of our core disciplines. My hope is that the ideas in this book will be a wake-up call for those growing numbers of kindred spirits who are ready to consider matters of the *soul*. The call is about fully claiming our spirituality, honoring it, weaving it into the fabric of our work. It is a call to acknowledge that our focus should be on the *sacred knowing* that our clients are whole human beings. It is a call to claim our spiritual life, the fire inside which drives our being human. It is a call to awaken to our own quest for meaning. Throughout the book, emphasis will be toward defining and describing the spiritual qualities of personal human experience and how these dimensions are integrated in a balanced and healthy human being.

The seeds of evolution toward a more inclusive and open attitude about our spiritual nature may be seen in the early through middle part of the twentieth century in the writings of such distinguished pioneer thinkers as Carl Jung, Alfred Adler, Paul Tillich, Rollo May, Victor Frankl, Eric Fromm, and Carl Rogers, among others. Even though these philosophers and psychologists dared to tread on such hollowed ground, they stepped lightly, being aware of the norms and boundaries of what could be accepted by their professional culture. Rogers, for example, did not speak directly about the power of "love" in his early work, he chose instead to call it unconditional positive regard. He knew intuitively that this language would be more readily acceptable within the norms of his peers. In his later years, Rogers (1980) did not concern himself about such possible censure and spoke more directly from his heart. He openly reported that his view had broadened: "... it seems that my inner spirit has reached out and touched the inner spirit of the other. Our relationship transcends itself and becomes part of something larger. Profound growth and healing energy are present." Although it wasn't "politically correct" at the time to frame it in such terms, I believe he was speaking about matters of our *soul*.

> *If the human soul is anything, it must be of unimaginable complexity and diversity.*
>
> — Carl Jung

❖ Major Forces of Resistance to the Study of the Soul: Religion and Science

Religion. Most of us in our culture have relegated, if not abdicated, our spiritual lives to our religious institutions. Our inner life is too often not examined or tapped for the wisdom that is available. We grow up with the idea that, "I don't have to think too much about my *soul* or matters of the spirit in my daily interactions because the church or temple, the ministers or priests or rabbis will take care of this for me." While millions will reserve a couple of hours each week of their busy schedules on their day of worship for a "spiritual (or religious) fix," this experience isn't always internalized and translated into their daily lives. The brevity, and the external focus of institutional devotion may in fact detract from more personal spiritual reflections and introspection so central to the quality of life. We delude ourselves if we believe that our spiritual life is outside our "self." This disconnect to the inner life of our *soul* is, I believe, one of the primary reasons for the sense of social anxiety so pervasive today.

Science. In our counseling professions, we have worked hard to gain the respect of the intellectual and scientific community, a culture that has strongly defined the boundaries of acceptable inquiry. The rules of the academic community in applied behavioral sciences focus on objectivity and that which can be most directly measured in specific cause-and-effect and/or statistically significant outcomes. As a result, our research and theoretical postulations in psychology have been primarily concerned with cognitive, behavioral, social and somatic themes. The psyche, or *soul*, had no acknowledgment within this traditional framework.

But more than twenty years ago, Fritjof Capra (1972) suggested that there is an imminent revolution in our perceptions and values, and that the old Cartesian method of analyzing the world into parts and cause-and-effect laws no longer gives a complete picture. He wrote:

> *What we need, then, is a new 'paradigm'; a new vision of reality; a fundamental change in our thoughts, perceptions, and values. The beginnings of this change, of the shift from the mechanistic to holistic conceptions of reality, are already visible in all fields and are likely to dominate the present decade.*

Capra described a general systems view of life: "the interrelatedness and interdependence of all phenomena — physical, biological, psychological, social and cultural." Corey (2005) validates this thinking in discussing the integration of eight "lenses" of family systems therapy. This integration of our multifaceted and unique selves is bound together by our *soul* consciousness. As awareness of the need for multicultural interdependency and global unity rise, a window has been opened for our profession to explore the differences and similarities our spirituality.

We are witnessing a renaissance of our human spirit in the helping professions. The voices which have argued that our work is more art than science, more intuitive than logical or sequential, and more wholistic* and integrated than parts or fragments, are being heard and respected.

I am writing about our *soul* because I believe it is the primary force in our lives, and as such, it behooves us as members of the helping professions, to address these most salient issues in our work. Readers are encouraged to peruse the Bibliography of this book to get just a small sampling of recent publications relating to these themes. Thousands of articles, and hundreds of books from such diverse existential and transpersonal writers as Norman

Cousins, Andrew Weil, Deepak Chopra and Bernie Siegel, are but a recent and short list of those who have moved us toward a vision of the power of our human spirit within.

And yet, virtually no one has addressed the concept of our human *soul* from the viewpoint taken in this book. While there has been much discussion in the psychological literature about the importance of "spirituality" in therapy, it has been mostly associated with religious beliefs. This book is, I believe, unique in exploring the importance of the client's inner life *(soul)* in counseling and therapy, how this bears upon the client's sense of meaning, and the choices clients have to actualize their natural human urge to grow and transcend their current dilemmas.

Our complex human experience defies the old and simplistic linear paradigms that have heretofore described our behavior. I see the eight ideas in the following list as fundamental to considerations of the *soul* as the center of our being.

Eight Assumptions about Human Experience

1. We are more than our thoughts
2. We are more than our emotions
3. We are more than our behavior
4. We are more than our physical bodies
5. There is a soul behind all these domains
6. All genuine compassion and caregiving comes from our soul which is the wellspring of love
7. Our soul considers all options for survival and development, and is the foundation of our choice making
8. As our soul is nourished, we gain in awareness of our self in relationships

---

As counselors, clinicians, social workers, and therapists of all persuasions, we must open our hearts to engage at the *soul* level with our clients who come to us with their quest for growth and their vulnerability. When we do this, we will arrive at a new understanding of the spiritual dimensions of our work. Such opening our hearts to another is a gift of supreme trust, and the foundation for all psychological healing. If we do not connect at a *soul* level in our care with our clients, with the love of acceptance, respect and compassion, we will be but symptom technicians, dealing with fragments of the person.

For those professionals working with clients who have physical maladies (nurses, physicians, physical therapists, occupational therapists, massage therapists, and others) a *soulful* connection is no less important. Even when the focus is primarily on physical considerations, clients will still be dealing with how their physical conditions will affect them in all their relationships and daily activities. There is no denying the totality of the person, nor the reality of a coherent consciousness.

My wish is for all readers to claim their own spirituality, to claim their own *soul*. The rest will follow. Let's put the *psyche* — which drives our total being — back in psychology.

> *Presumably qualities associated with spiritual development, such as energy, gentleness, joy, open-mindedness, generosity, patience, loving kindness, truthfulness and calm would be highly developed by a master.*
>
> — Frances Vaughn (1986)

A word about style: Throughout this book, I have adopted a number of stylistic conveniences that reflect my commitment to a soul-centered view of the counseling process. Here are two of those author liberties:

1. *I have attempted in this work to retain a perspective that is both personal and universal. When I'm describing human characteristics that I believe to be true of all of us, and often when I'm discussing the qualities of an individual client, I use the plural pronouns of "we" and "our." I hope this will not be confusing to the reader. I consider it very important that we as counseling professionals acknowledge our own humanness along with that of our clients.*

2. I use the spelling "wholistic" because it speaks to the whole person, rather than "holistic," which may suggest a religious quality of being "holy."

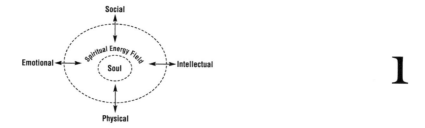

The Emperor's Clothes
Something Is Missing

Like the loyal subjects praising the naked emperors' fashionable attire, we as faithful professionals have also blindly followed the authority and traditions of the established hierarchy. We have revered western science and avoided anything that couldn't be demonstrated at the .01 level of confidence in predicting outcomes. While some brave *souls* secretly granted that *love* is the basis of acceptance, respect, empathy, and compassion, most pretended not to see it. For them the focus was on the measured and precise outcomes of science. In spite of this tunnel vision, our earlier pioneers in psychology laid the groundwork for us to understand the motivations, the manifestations and the consequences of human behavior. While they all shared their theories of counseling and human experience in brilliant and compelling ways, it is alarming to think that the twentieth century has been one of bickering about which theory of counseling has the *"right way."*

Most major theories of counseling fall somewhere within the realm of the reciprocating four-dimensional model as shown below.

When anything went wrong with any of the parts of a person as a functioning being, each specialist looked at the person and her or his struggles through the filter of a particular theoretical lens. It was a little like adjusting the specific parts of the engine of a car, when the problem was with the quality of the combustible fuel. Very little has been said or done by theorists about the fuel,

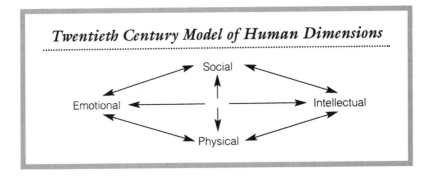

or *energy* which drives the physical, social, emotional and intellectual dimensions of human behavior. We forget that it is the wisdom of our integrated being that heals. I will try to make the case that this energy comes from our *soul*, our essential being.

Theories of human development that have explained the rationale of each of the four dimensions are all defined and encapsulated within the self-imposed limits of the traditional scientific method. None of the theories are really connected with the idea of *soul*. Any theory that hinted at something like a *soul* or spiritual dimension never saw the light of day in modern psychology. As a consequence, our theories have been too concerned with techniques and methods, and — with the exception of Carl Rogers' (1961) and Carl Jung (1958) — each missed the heart of the matter. About the closest other theorists came to acknowledging the essential spirit of the client was in paying perfunctory lip service to the necessity of establishing rapport. Carl Jung observed: "... that the human psyche seeks integration and that there is an instinctual drive toward wholeness and health." While his voice resonates throughout the development of the professions, many of his thoughts on spirituality have failed to make the mainstream of human services curricula.

❖ Heart and Soul

> *The best and most beautiful things*
> *In the world cannot be seen or even touched,*
> *They must be felt with the heart*
> — Helen Keller

The lyrics and title of the old song *"Heart & Soul"* tie our imaginations to the idea that *soul* is more a matter of the heart than a function of the mind. Poets and musicians somehow know this intuitively, and it is their creative expressions that touch us so deeply at the core of our being. One example of this is the Tin Man from *The Wizard of Oz* singing, "If I only had a heart," bemoaning his lack of heart as the only thing that kept him from being human.

The missing link in counseling has been that we have not acknowledged the *heart* and *soul* of a person. This core of our being creates our energy field, fuels our vitality, and directs our thoughts, feelings, and actions, defining our sense of self.

We often say that something wonderful someone said or did is "heartfelt," but we rarely look beyond the figure of speech to see that the word is truly a bridge, lending common understanding to the meaning of spiritual experience.

The "eight elements" shown in the list below offer some thoughts on the matter of defining soul and how it relates to our work.

Eight Elements of Soul Awareness

1. **I am alive; I exist as a separate being**
   This is my sense of self that manifests my unique lifeforce.
   It is the inner "I" in me that is the truth beyond ego or social mask.
2. **I need love.** My greatest satisfaction comes when I am giving and receiving compassionate understanding with those I love.
3. **I need to belong to a family and a community.**
   I realize we are all here to help each other, and to make the world a better place.
4. **I have awareness about my senses and what I perceive.** My physical being is sacred.
5. **I can learn, and I have choices about my behaviors, attitudes and beliefs.**
6. **I have feelings (emotions)** related to all the above.
7. **I continue to be open to experience, to meaning, and to purpose,** questing for integration, for wellness, and for happiness.
8. **I stand in awe of the universe,** and the knowing that I am part of it.

Being Human

I am more than my body, or my mind,
more than emotions or thoughts,
more than my social engagements,
I am a self, a soul a whole person
There is a lifeforce within me
with a will to survive,
a need to love and be loved,
and a questing for meaning and purpose

— dw

❖ *Common Sense and Experience*

I feel strongly that, as human services professionals, we need to think seriously about *soul* issues, observing how they might be manifest, and claiming our spiritual nature in describing what we observe and experience. Because we can see and feel this life force energy in ourselves and in relationship to others, we can build a framework of understanding of how *soul* interfaces in our relationships in counseling and human services. We know in fields of applied psychology, as well as by our common sense, that it is our human relationships that nourish our *soul*. This is the *self*, making meaning out of the context of our lives. For example, we know that our individual well-being is founded in a sense of belonging within family, friends and community, where we are loved, accepted, acknowledged and valued. Within or without the richness of this context, we seek a sense of self, an identity of who we are, and try to gain meaning from the question: *"What is my life about?"*

Bringing these *soul* matters into a tangible perspective and a viable theory for delivering human services, we must acknowledge this neglected dimension of our essential being as the central meaning-maker in our lives. We need to recognize all the observable manifest behavior such as caring, respect, trust, and hope (or their opposites) as *soul* indicators. We need also to make a case that our *soul* exists apart from mysticism or religion.

I presented a paper (1995) in Ireland entitled, *Claiming our Spirituality: Teachable, Tangible, and Too Long in the Closet.* It was my first attempt to say to counselors in training that we need to recognize and honor our spiritual essence as the energy core that mediates our intellectual, our emotional, our social and our physiological dimensions of behavior.

The following model acknowledges this essential core element of the self.

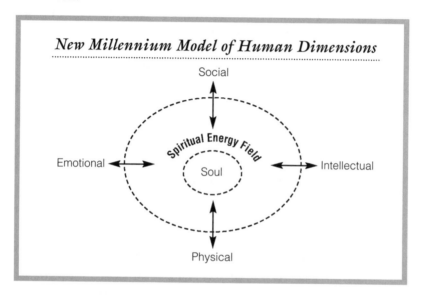

New Millennium Model of Human Dimensions

In this model, our *soul,* our consciousness of "self." is at the center of our total external expression. From this core of our being comes what I call a spiritual energy field. This is the domain in which decisions are made, values are shaped and held, and our ability to love and to be loved may be found.

It is clear that we are more than our rationality, more than our emotion, more than our social relationships, sexuality, or behavior. We are more than our attitudes and values, more than our nationality, our race or our religion. At the level of our *soul,* we know that we are a unique configuration of all these components and more in a context of our history, our multiple subcultures, our genetic heritage, and our hopes and dreams.

❖ *A Major Shortfall*

As I have emphasized, in counseling and other human services training programs we have been very negligent with respect to matters of the *soul* in human experience. Little has been written about expressions of our human spirit for use in human services training classrooms. Our graduate programs in counseling psychology, psychotherapy, and social work have been and continue to be diligent in trying to endow our profession with scientific credibility. In much of the twentieth century, anything as ethereal as *soul* was not encouraged as viable academic pursuit.

The old adage, "I wouldn't touch it with a ten foot pole," fits well in describing our attitude about confronting the human spirit in the academic world of psychology. It just hasn't been safe. It is not safe because it's not rewarded, and academic freedom is compromised. Historically, pursuit of matters of the human spirit has been a dead-end-alley in the academic world of applied behavioral sciences. Other fields of academic endeavor, such as philosophy, literature, art, music and religion have not been so constrained in discussing *soul* issues.

> *It is easier to reorganize a graveyard*
> *Than it is to change higher education*
> — Warren Bennis

❖ *Acknowledging the Spiritual Field*

Carl Rogers (1961) came the closest to attending to matters of the *soul* in his person-centered approach in counseling; he just didn't label it as *soul*. The norms of the professional culture at that time didn't offer support or encouragement to discuss love or any matters that might invite leaving the hallowed grounds of western science. In spite of this inhibiting factor, Rogers courageously laid the groundwork for us to see the *self* behind the symptoms, the person in spiritual process. He knew that to gain acceptance and viability, he would have to use terms more amenable to the behavioral sciences of his time, so he called love "unconditional positive regard." Perfect for the time! He gave us the gift of seeing how congruence, transparency, genuineness, warmth, acceptance, and belief in the power within each person to realize her or his full potential are essential conditions to the unfolding of individuals on their path toward health and well-being. Rogers's emphasis on listening and responding to the core meaning of the person showed us all how to pay attention to the deeper *soul* issues of human experience. He made empathy tangible, and placed it at the center of our work.

The acceptance of Rogers's approach got a major boost from the scientific research of Truax and Carkhuff (1967), among others. These two researchers in particular dissected the process of reflective listening and demonstrated that there are quantifiable differences in the quality of the counselor's response. Empathy was seen differentially and judged by experts for quality of response. While this was a major contribution in support of person-centered theory, it failed to look beyond the behaviorally scientific to the more illusive assumptions of the touching of human spirit or *soul* connection between counselor and client. The academic culture was simply not ready for such an imaginative translation of the evidence.

Earlier, Alfred Adler had also addressed *soul* issues without calling them such. Throughout his major works, Adler wrote about purpose, meaning, choice, creativity, social interest, community feeling, equality, encouragement, and caring for others. These powerful ideas, so clearly an expression of our human spirit, had a great impact on the field of psychology, but the academic and professional culture of his time was also not ready to frame this work as spiritual. Most other writers of spiritual considerations, including Roberto Assagioli (1965) and the approach he called *psychosynthesis*, never made the mainstream. Assagioli did make significant contributions and challenged us to broaden our perspectives, asserting that "spiritual drives or spiritual urges are... real, basic and fundamental (p. 194)." Rollo May (1991), Viktor Frankl (1959), Paul Tillich (1952), Martin Buber (1970), Eric Fromm (1956) and many other existential writers of the twentieth century created the groundwork and enhanced our understanding of our quest for meaning. They all wrote of *self*, freedom and, ultimately, *soul*.

As counselors and therapists we acknowledge and honor our clients' feelings, inviting them to explore and to get to the "heart" of the matter. Even as we listen to the story beneath or behind these feelings, it is particularly ironic that we have failed to acknowledge the *soul* connection, since the essence of who we are is expressed from our *psyche*. It is imperative that we understand this in our work in human services because the very act of any therapeutic intervention arises from our inner spirit of caring. Where else? Clients come to us looking for acknowledgment, acceptance, respect and encouragement, all spiritual elements and manifestations of compassion. To consider counseling outside of this *soulful* context renders it more in the realm of technique, methodology, or clever intervention. There is something cold, calculating and categorical when we attempt to explain and predict human behavior with linear, logical, sequential and systematic paradigms, and fail to acknowledge the more unique, personal and *soulful* human elements. Carl Jung (1958) put it this way...

> *There are ways which bring us nearer to living experience, yet we should beware of calling these ways 'methods.' The very word has a deadening effect. The way to experience, moreover, is anything but a clever trick; it is rather a venture which requires us to commit ourselves with our whole being.*

When we commit ourselves with our whole being, our compassion resonates deeply in relationships, and is beyond technique, systems or methods. It is in compassion that we find the seeds for healing the wounds of our human spirit. When we genuinely connect with our clients, we experience an encounter of our *souls*. Our job as counselors is to help our clients discover their own inner wisdom, their spiritual field, and how to tap into it. One important aspect for developing spirituality is by enhancing healthy relationships and a sense of belonging within a community of family and friends.

Consciousness Rising

We have entered this millennium with a greater sense of freedom to consider spiritual ideas. It was heartening to note that the theme of the 2001 convention of the American Counseling Association (ACA) was "Celebration of Our Human Spirit." One of the major reasons we as professionals in human service are more ready to consider spiritual matters is because of the rising wave of consciousness concerning multicultural issues. This movement has helped us claim our differences with pride in the origins and traditions of our many diverse racial and ethnic heritages. It has enhanced our respect and tolerance for spiritual diversity as well.

A good example of this is found in a book chapter by Michael James Yellowbird (2000) entitled "Spirituality in First Nations Storytelling: A Sahnish-Hidatsa Approach to Narrative." He tells us that storytelling is the primary way to keep traditions alive. Elders pass on their perspectives with stories and create a sense of purpose and belonging. He writes: "Indeed, telling our history reminds us of who we are, where we came from, and what we should expect from our future." He claims that personal narratives remind tribal members of... "their identity and purpose in life and death." In his summary, he suggests that, when elders share their personal narratives, "This traditional approach teaches the village membership about humility, respect and patience" (p. 123). Are not all these qualities from the essence of our spirit?

❖ *Name It and Claim It*

To acknowledge our spiritual dimensions by naming them and claiming them as such in our everyday language is to honor our deepest meaning and our highest aspirations. It is to acknowledge that our feelings, attitudes, thoughts and actions are coming from a *sacred* place within us. Because our spirits are expressed in tangible ways, we are on somewhat safer turf with respect to more traditional measurement methods in the social sciences. We can point to and define our terms in observable behaviors and we have a growing body of research evidence that supports our claims.

Vaillant (1977) examined the linkage between love and health by following 200 Harvard graduates for thirty years. He found that, "The Healthier men reflected a friendlier disposition and closer relationships with their children, were happily married over time and revealed better sexual adjustment." He concluded that being able to love ones friends, wife, parents and children were predictors of good mental health. (p. 145)

Witmer and Sweeney (1992) suggest that "This [Vaillant] study and the others reported support the position that trust, intimacy, caring, companionship, compassion and similar qualities of a loving relationship promote good health and longevity" (p. 145). In reporting on their model for spiritual wellness they write, "We define 'spirituality' independently of 'religion', that is, spirituality can occur in or out of the context of organized religion, and not all aspects of religion are assumed to be spiritual" (p. 120).

❖ *Not a Church and State Issue*

Organized religion is, and has been for perhaps most of us, our introduction to and our primary arena for, defining and discussing spirituality. But as thoughtful adults, we all know that it is not the only avenue to our inner selves. My intention is not to take issue with any religion or faith, it is simply to lay claim to our spiritual expressions that may be found in everyday *life outside as well as within* our places of worship. Religion has been and continues to be a very important dimension of the spiritual lives of millions of people *but it must not be seen as the sole custodian of the language of our human spiritual experiences.* Because we have relegated so much of our spiritual lives to the domain of religion, matters of the inner life of our human spirit have been largely ignored in the schools and other tax-supported human service agencies. It is important that we not throw the spiritual baby out with the religious bath water.

This book is about expressing our spiritual lives in ways that do not exclude any person and do not take issue with any religion. There is no seeking of converts, no dogma or doctrine which preaches that this is the only way, or even the best way. There is no discussion or focus on external deities or mysticism. There is no violation of the constitutional amendment regarding separation of church and state because spiritual development in human experience is addressed apart from any religion.

As professional counselors and therapists, we need to lay aside some of our academic knowledge base — logic, sequence, rationality — as we reflect and balance this dimension with our more intuitive and spiritual side. In a way, we need to return to our more childlike innocence where our sensing is more global, our hunches less fixed, our imagination of possibilities more open. Too many of our professional hierarchical accoutrements only get in the way of creating a *"soul"* connection, person-to-person. This does not mean throwing out the professional and ethical judgments and perspectives gained from our knowledge and skill training. It simply means finding a more sensible balance between the brain's right and left hemispheres. As counselors, the spiritual dimension is the most authentic arena for our work. We need to incorporate the tangible spiritual expressions of our human experience (such as love, compassion, tenderness, warmth, caring and respect) into our professional and personal lives. All counseling is spiritual. How could it be otherwise?

We Hunger and Thirst
for Authenticity

Our soul cries out to be real
And to still be loved
To be free
And still belong
To be grateful
But not obliged
What are the chances
Of being so whole?

We wear masks
To hide ourselves from
ourselves and others
To be accepted
We wonder...
Could others love us
If they really knew us?

I say...better to be known
And risk judgment
Than to be not known
Playing it safe.

— dw

Soul Searching Journal Assignments — for Your Clients and for Yourself

❖

- Write your thoughts about how the *Eight Elements of Soul Awareness* might apply in your life.
- Should Do *vs.* Want To Do: Listen to your inner voice of *soul*, which mediates and guides your choices as you struggle between what you think you ought to do, and what you know you want to do. Write in your journal, giving expression to your *should* as well as to your *want to*, voices. Express these voices having a dialogue. Invite your logical, your emotional, and your cultural voices to get into the mix as you open up to working out choices in your dilemmas.
- How does your *soul* as the ultimate decision maker relate to your state of health and overall well-being?
- How do your religious beliefs interface with your beliefs about your personal *soul* expressions?

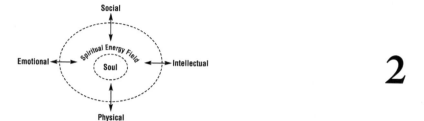

Soul in Everyday Life

My spirit and your spirit are what ultimately define us: it is our spirit that gives meaning and direction to our experience, it is our spirit that determines our identity and it is our spirit which bears the mark of mortality. We are body, mind and spirit but it is the spirit that breathes life and gives light — or colludes, with death and darkness. The existentialists' question: 'who am I?' can only be satisfactorily answered in terms of the spirit.

— Brian Thorne (1988)

Before we go on discuss the role of *soul* in counseling, let's take a look at the concept of *soul* in a broader context. What is the *soul*, anyway? How does *soul* manifest itself in everyday experience?

Conventional wisdom tells us that we have a *soul*. Webster's Dictionary defines *soul* as: "that immaterial essence, animating principle or actuating cause of an individual life." Most of us accept that we have a "consciousness of the cosmos," and that we are capable of experiencing love and wonder. Here is an attempt to define what I believe about my *soul* as it is expressed as that animating principle or activating cause:

Soul is the essence of who we are
Our inner wisdom... if we learn to listen
Our pilot as we quest for meaning and purpose
And bear witness in wonder
At the sacred mystery of it all
Soul is the source of our spiritual energy
We see it in each other's eyes, and posture
Hear it in our tones of voice
The fiber of our soul is in our every act
Our language; our music and dance, our work
  and our recreation
All creativity arises from our soul

— dw

As I've pointed out before, I am defining *soul* and *spirituality* as separate from religion or mysticism. While millions will find their spiritual guidance in various religious institutions, those of us who may not affiliate with a particular religious persuasion also have *souls* and concerns about spiritual matters. The *soul* about which I write is universal, knowing no boundaries between religions, denominations or sects.

When we consider significant experiences in our lives, we quickly see that these most often involve relationships, and that there is a spiritual quality in those relationships that resonates deeply within us. Birth, marriage, family, life, and death are examples of profoundly spiritual experiences, all of which are about our self and the people we love. These are some of the life experiences of the *soul* that generate our spirituality and bring meaning to our lives. Rachel Kessler (2000) writes that *soul* is about our inner life, and about finding meaning, purpose and connection. In her book, *The Soul of Education*, she points out that there is a longing for more than the ordinary, material, and fragmented existence.

If we think of events that involve tragedy and crisis — the death of a child, disability from an accident or illness, on-going abuse, addiction to alcohol or other drugs, suicide or criminal behavior — we realize these experiences powerfully impact our human spirit. These are not just emotional issues, nor can they be solved just with our intellect. These are matters that affect our whole being because of the *psychic* insult. These are truly wounds to our *souls*.

People who come to us for counseling often feel disconnected from significant relationships in family, marriage, and the workplace. Like the rest of us, they hunger for acknowledgment, validation, acceptance, caring, encouragement and intimacy. Notice the spiritually nourishing qualities of these words. All too often these experiences are missing in the lives of those persons we call clients.

❖ *Frenetic Gathering*

We all hunger for belonging, for acceptance and for acknowledgment. We all want to love and be loved. So often these matters of our human spirit are overshadowed by our distorted notion that material success is our most important achievement. To the extent that we are caught up in this quest for gathering, we have not yet transcended the mouse in the maze looking for the cheese. We lock ourselves in our own prison of obsession when we leave our search for meaning for the path of most material return. When priorities shift from love to over-achievement, the spiritual cost to us is enormous, often measured in the loss of friendships, of family love, or compromised principles. This frenetic gathering is only a symptom of our deeper longing for love and spiritual bonding with our fellow human beings.

❖ *Our Spiritual Energy Field*

Our vitality is drawn from our spiritual energy field. It is the source of our values, beliefs, attitudes, and that unique persona that directs our choices and behaviors. We all know people who express a very up-beat "sunshine" personality: enthusiastic, optimistic, trusting, open, encouraging and friendly. We also know others who are more subdued, but with *spiritual qualities* of sincerity, genuineness and sensitivity as their strengths. All these qualities will be expressed in different ways under different circumstances.

We may see clients coming to us feeling down and perhaps desperate, with but dim spiritual vitality. For example, Phil had closed himself off from dating, because he was fearful of ever trusting a woman again. While he desired companionship and intimacy, he was paralyzed with ambivalence and by the fear of being hurt and betrayed again. Opening his heart to admit his hurt and fear allowed him to soften his rigid and polarized attitude. The differences between these polarities in *spiritual energy field* are defined by whether or not one has received love, caring, acceptance and validation of one's essential goodness as a human being. This manifest love is particularly important in infancy and early years of development. When we get quality love in our early years, our spirit becomes "imprinted"(just like the duckling's first sighting of a mother object), and the strength of it stays with us. Even with this early love, we all need to be validated and cared about throughout the span of our lives if we are to keep the spark of our spirit alive. When the *soul* is well nourished, the human spirit is radiant. We are warmed by the spunk, the grit, the good cheer, the love, the laughter, and the friendship, of such "good *souls.*" The list below offers a quick alphabetical listing of some positive samples for such expression.

Soul Experiences Which Nourish and Sustain Our Spiritual Energy Field

Acceptance and Affirmation	Negotiation
Beauty and Bounty	Openness
Caring and Compassion	Pleasure
Delight	Quality Relationships
Encouragement	Responsibility
Friendship and Family	Sharing
Gratitude	Togetherness
Humility	Unity
Ideals & Imagination	Vitality
Justice	Wonder
Kindness	eXcellence and eXuberance
Love	Yearning
Marriage	Zest

Our *souls* are nourished and expressed within the experiences of everyday life. Let me pose to you some common sense questions to illuminate this point. Check all that may apply to you:

__ Does your human spirit respond to enthusiasm?

__ Does it bear upon your vitality?

__ Can it be communicated non-verbally?

__ Does it involve respect?

__ Does it involve valuing?

__ Does it affect your decisions?... your attitudes?... your belief system?... your desire?... your behavior?

__ Is it love?

__ Is it tenderness?

__ Is it caring?

If you answered all questions with a "yes," you can give yourself an "E" for enlightenment and another "E" for excellence. You have come to know that our human spirit is the glue in all we do. The *soul* is not as hidden away, nor as mysterious as we might have thought. It is our *soul* which permeates our every thought, feeling and action. When I reflect about some of my own *soul* experiences, I think of times like these...

... sitting under the stars on a clear night

... being in nature, at the ocean or lake or in the woods or fields

... enjoying music, dance or sports

... playing and laughing with friends

... savoring close family time.

I believe most people find in these, and many other similar experiences, a deep *soul* resonance within.

❖ *"Soul Music"*
━━━━━━━━━━━━━━━━━━━━━━━━━━━━━━━━━━━━━━━

Music is a moral law. It gives wings to the mind, soul to the universe, flight to the imagination, charm to sadness, and life to everything.

— Plato

Music can be a particularly powerful experience for me. There have been times when I have been moved to tears by a song or a symphony, and other times of great joy and exuberance singing and playing music with friends and family. When my sons and I get together, we sing and play. Dave and Chris hold forth on the guitar, Michael picks up his harmonica, John the bass and I my banjo. Together we blend our voices, and it is total joy. Sometimes one of my good buddies, Bert or Wiggie, will be on the piano, with Will providing the heartbeat with his drums. These times produce their own moments of magic. Each player-singer initiating a song or two in turn, others chiming in with their instruments and voices, all in harmony. It is such a burst of joyful love and *soul*ful spontaneity! I am blessed with other gatherings more in a folk-music arena with Greg, David, or Paul, for some oldies-but-goodies. Every October at the peak of foliage, we gather at Fort Dwight, our mountain retreat on the Kancamagas, in the White Mountains of New Hampshire. This event brings together all the Ordway-Hallett Raiders — our two generations of mountain hikers and musicians — to resonate the rafters with our hoots and hollers. Straight from the heart and *soul*, this band of balladeers produces some truly outstanding songs and stories. It's a great tradition that I believe will warm those timbers for many generations to come.

❖ The Verbal and Non-Verbal Language of the Soul

Our *soul* shines through our eyes and the warmth of our smiles, our openness and our cheerful greetings. Our spirit may be read easily in our tone of voice and our body posture. Our spirit is expressed in our wholeness and is the essence of our being fully human. Unspoken and spoken language is our great bridge for sharing who we are.

The meaning of words that are essentially spiritual in nature goes far beyond cognition, emotion or behavior. For example: If I have faith in someone, and they know it, they feel encouraged by my confidence in them. Words like faith, encouragement and confidence describe experiences of our *soul*. The word *encourage* comes from the Latin root word for heart and may be defined as, "to inspire with courage, spirit or hope; to hearten and spur on."

We have a perfectly adequate vocabulary to use for framing our thoughts of everyday life experience in the spiritual domain. Love is, of course, our most encompassing term, and in a sense, its presence or lack of presence is fundamental to all acts of our spirit. It is easy enough to see that compassion, tenderness, warmth, caring, kindness, and gratitude all stem from love. When we experience being accepted, understood, appreciated and acknowledged in a very personal and genuine way, we are touched and we are moved. These observable acts of love are tangible, forceful, peaceful, and stimulating as they express our human spirit in simple, natural and often profound ways.

 ### *Wounds of the Human Spirit*

When love is absent in our lives, our spirits will be dampened down as swiftly and surely as the fire in a wood stove when the flue closes out oxygen. Toxic messages and actions wreak severe damage to our human *soul*. We have all had an experience when it felt like someone threw a wet blanket on our enthusiasm. When our zest for life has been discouraged, or if we have been rejected, put-down, ignored, or in any other way abused or neglected, our spirits are negatively impacted. The consequences of these wounds will vary by the severity of the abuse, the strength of our support system (network of love and caring), and our own spiritual strength.

I remember being hurt by a remark from my grandfather when I was about ten years old. He was a carpenter, and I was trying to saw a straight line on board to be cut. He said something like, "You don't have it, Dwight. Your older brother Loren has it, but you just don't have it to be a carpenter." It's interesting that I still remember it six decades, three house designs, millions of nails, and a thousand boards cut, later. Lately, when I'm doing carpentry with my friend Paul, I tell him how my grandfather would be proud of me each time I make a nice fit on something, *and we laugh*. I think I've just about worked through this insult. I suppose that's making lemon-aid out of lemons, but it was still a wet blanket that I didn't appreciate. I never felt close to my grandfather after that really, and this was a very mild example of abuse. I guess I was a pretty sensitive lad.

While Sir Isaac Newton was the first to observe that *for every action there is an equal and opposite reaction,* in psychology we are not immune to these laws of physics. Human development also deals with energy, and we see, for example, that for every social action there is an equal-intensity reaction. Our responses are expressed either inwardly or outwardly when we are in relationship to another being. Certainly we are impacted when someone insults us or puts us down. How we cope with these wounds is the concern of parents, educators, counselors, and other professional caregivers.

A Sampling of Words Describing How We Might Feel if Negative Spiritual Energy Is Directed Toward Us

abused	diminished	inadequate	powerless
aggravated	disabled	incapable	prejudiced
agitated	disagreeable	incompetent	puny
angry	discounted	ineffective	put down
annoyed	discredited	inefficient	rebellious
antagonistic	disdained	inept	reckless
belittled	disgraced	inferior	resentful
belligerent	disparaged	insecure	revengeful
bigoted	disregarded	insensitive	ridiculed
broken down	enraged	insufficient	sadistic
callous	exposed	intolerant	scorned
cantankerous	feeble	irritated	shaken
censured	fragile	mad	shamed
combative	frail	malicious	slandered
contrary	furious	maligned	slighted
criticized	gruesome	mean	small
cross	hard-hearted	meek	spiteful
cruel	harsh	minimized	trivial
debilitated	hateful	neglected	uncertain
defamed	heartless	obstinate	underestimated
defective	helpless	oppositional	unfit
deficient	hostile	oppressed	unfriendly
deflated	humiliated	outraged	unimportant
demoralized	ignored	overlooked	unqualified
derided	ill-tempered	perturbed	unsound

Other Words Associated with Depression, Fear and Anxiety

abandoned	discouraged	hated	pathetic
afraid	disgusted	hopeless	perplexed
alienated	disliked	humiliated	rebuked
anxious	dismal	impaired	rejected
apathy	distrustful	insecure	reprimanded
apprehensive	disregarded	intimidated	terrified
battered	dreadful	jealous	timid
beaten	estranged	lost	tormented
betrayed	excluded	miserable	unhappy
bewildered	fearful	mistreated	unloved
debased	forlorn	offended	unsatisfied
degraded	forsaken	ostracized	unsure
despised	futile	overwhelmed	violated
devastated	grim	panicky	worthless

Boys Flying Kites,
Haul in their white winged birds
You can't do that
when you're flying words

Careful with fire
is good advice we know
careful with words
is ten times doubly so

Words unexpressed
sometimes fall back dead,
but even God can't kill them
once they are said

— Unknown

Here is a *soul*-healing exercise for your clients that you may want to try yourself. Recall a negative experience that came your way and write a brief sentence, or key words and names of persons to bring it up on your memory screen. Then challenge the negative hold this experience has had on you and write, or say, "I will no longer give my power away to this. I don't deserve it, and I don't want it." Take a deep breath, crumple the paper, exhale, and say or write: "I don't need this anymore." Then throw the crumpled paper into the wastebasket. Such deliberate acts of affirmation will begin to re-program your patterned negative thoughts.

It is this symbolic acting out to complete unfinished business that is healing to our *soul*. It is a Gestalt idea of challenging previously untouched negative material, and integrating it into a more wholistic perspective. It is a reclaiming of personal power which had been given away. And it is a very useful tool in counseling.

To claim our childhood innocence and our basic goodness, we need a beginner's mind that lets go of fixed attitudes, and opens to love and the belief that there are those who care. We will come to forgive those who have hurt us because of their own wounded *souls*, and as we do, we come to an acceptance of our own shortcomings.

A Sampling of Words of Positive Spiritual Energy Associated with Health and Well Being

able	competent	effective	friendly
adequate	confident	elated	gallant
agreeable	congenial	empathetic	generous
amiable	considerate	empowered	genuine
assured	contented	energetic	giving
authoritative	cooperative	enthusiastic	glad
blissful	courageous	exalted	glorious
bold	daring	excellent	good
brave	dedicated	excited	grand
brilliant	delighted	fair	gratified
calm	determined	faithful	great
capable	devoted	fantastic	happy
caring	dynamic	fine	hardy
cheerful	easy-going	fit	healthy
comforting	ecstatic	forgiving	helpful

(cont'd.)

honest	mighty	respectful	sure
honorable	neighborly	responsible	sympathetic
hospitable	nice	robust	tender
humane	open	secure	terrific
humorous	optimistic	self-confident	thoughtful
important	patient	self-reliant	thrilled
inspired	peaceful	sensitive	tolerant
interested	pleasant	serene	trustworthy
joyous	pleased	sharp	truthful
just	polite	skillful	understanding
kind	powerful	splendid	unselfish
lovable	proud	stable	virile
loving	reasonable	stouthearted	vivacious
magnificent	receptive	strong	witty
marvelous	reliable	superb	wonderful

❖ *The Power of Love*

When we experience an act of love, whether it is a compliment, encouragement, appreciation, or some other expression of another's love and prizing of us, we are nourished. These acts might include a physical gesture, such as a hug, an arm around the shoulder, a smile and friendly eye contact. Such spontaneous expressions from a person's spirit touch us instantly. Our vitality and the motivation that drives us in such complex ways cannot really be expressed in words alone. Acts of love are always the more powerful expression. Demonstrative affection is particularly important in infancy through adolescence, but tangible expressions of love must be in supply all of our lives if we are to thrive, and move toward our potential.

> *And when I just don't know*
> *which way the wind will blow*
> *no one else can ease my mind*
> *you see rainbows I can't find.*
> *...So many times you've been a mirror to my soul*
> *lighting up the shadows, making me whole.*
>
> — Susan Joy (1973)

Soul Searching Journal Assignments — for Your Clients, and for Yourself

- Define what *soul* means to you.
- How is your balance between your interest in material goods and the quality of your inner spiritual life?
- Write the name of the person who comes to mind for each word on the list of *Soul Experiences Which Nourish and Sustain Our Spiritual Energy Field.*
- Write about a wound to your spirit, and your current stage of resolution of that wound.
- Using all the vocabulary lists, put a check mark (✓) by those that most resonate with you. Then go back and write a sentence or two on each, focusing on what memories and experiences get triggered, and what they mean to you now.
- Ask yourself questions: Who do I need to forgive? What do I need to let go of? What is keeping me from letting go? What are my edges of growth? How do I get there?

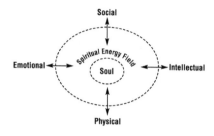

Toward a Theory of Soul
in Counseling

Where does consciousness come from?
What is the psyche?
At this point, all science ends.
           — Carl Jung (1933)

The word *psyche* (which means *soul*) is the root of the word *psychology* — the study of the *soul*. It is interesting that we have largely overlooked and abandoned this meaning in our academic endeavors in psychology.

In our training as counselors we have focused our attention on our clients' stories, their history and the context of their lives. We have been told to be concerned with their cognitive responses, their *self*-talk and their beliefs about how life "should" be. We have been taught to challenge our clients through behavioral interventions and to encourage emotional catharsis and free association. All of these approaches have merit and meaning, and all contribute value to a greater understanding of the whole person. But there has been a major shortfall!

In our desire to be theoretically correct and well-founded in our knowledge bases, we sometimes lose sight of the fact that our clients bring to us their hunger for meaning and purpose, for genuineness, authenticity and intimacy, a yearning for family stability, and for marriages that are happy and strong. All these elements are rooted in and reflect our human spirit. All are matters of our *soul*. The reason we don't see the connection of this longing for meaning to our *psyche* or *soul* is that the relationship between our *soul* and our experience has never been clearly identified in our professional training or practice.

John Welwood (2000) writes:

> *Freud once admitted, in a letter to Jung 'that psychoanalysis is essentially a cure through love.' While psychotherapists might privately agree that love has some kind of role in the healing process, the word "love" is curiously absent from most of the therapeutic literature. The same is true for the word "heart." Not only is this term missing from the psychological literature, the tone of the literature itself also lacks heart.*

Because our consciousness of spirituality in counseling has been expanding so rapidly as we have entered the new millennium, our professional culture has a window of opportunity open for the development of a theory base which more directly addresses matters of our human spirit.

> *Spirituality is less a method than an attitude, a posture of one's being that allows seeing not different things, but everything differently.*
>
> — Ernest Kurtz (1999)

Webster's dictionary defines theory as "*a plausible or scientifically acceptable general principle or body of principles offered to explain a phenomenon.*" I like the word *plausible* in this definition better than the term *scientifically acceptable* because it invites more imagination. It's not that science need not apply in matters of the *soul*, it's just that we should not allow ourselves to create rigid categories which limit the scope of our thinking regarding human behavior. We can't, and shouldn't, attempt to reduce human experience to narrow categories. Not everything can be reduced to numbers. The language of poetry and metaphor, for example, can communicate profound meaning, as can music, theater, and other expressive arts, drawing us toward the resonating truth of common experience.

Theories give us a framework, with reference points around which we can share ideas. They provide the tools for our work and serve as a foundation and a reservoir for our thoughtful responses with our clients. Theories need to have fluidity, a kind of breathing-in and breathing-out flexibility that can expand with creative thinking. A theory that involves *soul* will require a willingness to suspend our pre-ordained ideas, and have an openness of our minds toward that which is new and uncertain. Although the essence of *soul* is much too pervasive to be reduced to the requirements of scientific measurement, we nonetheless need to build a coherent foundation of understanding about how human behavior emerges from our human spirit.

Four Basic Tenets for The Soul of Counseling

Webster's defines the word tenet as "*a principle, belief or doctrine generally held to be true; especially: one held in common with the members of an organization, group, movement or profession.*"

I believe we can come to a reasonable agreement on tenets of the *soul* as they relate to the common purposes of our work in human services. The following tenets, upon which a theory of *soul* in counseling could be based, are grounded in common sense and experience, and are not cast in stone. It is my hope that they will be studied and expanded to enhance and further clarify the meanings and implications of each, as our understanding grows.

TENET I   ... **Within each of us there is a *soul*; an awareness of *self* as an autonomous being.**

TENET II ... **Our *soul* mediates all of our thoughts, feelings, choices and actions.**

TENET III... **Human life depends on love.**

TENET IV ... **All life seeks to survive and to fulfill itself.**

Let's take a look at each of these four tenets in light of their implications for counseling and allied human services.

TENET I... Within each of us there is a soul; *an awareness of self as an autonomous being.*

The organism in its normal state, moves toward its own fulfillment, toward self-regulation, and independent from external control.

— Carl Rogers

Carl Rogers (1961) had it right in developing his person-centered approach. He writes: "First of all, the client moves toward being autonomous." He goes on to say that, as clients move toward self-direction and personal responsibility, they move away from meeting others' expectations, away from *shoulds* and *oughts*, and away from behaving in ways intended just to please another person. Rogers speaks of the *true self* emerging as the façade is shed. This is a powerful declaration, acknowledging the inner life of the person. I dare say we could call this inner life of the *true self* our *soul.*

It is our *soul* that yearns to be loved, to be acknowledged, accepted, and cared for. It is our *soul* that stands up to outside oppression. It is our *soul* that bears the brunt of our reality. It is our *soul* that wants to dance and to sing. We see all these manifestations magnified in our children as they develop and find their way. A child whose *soul* is not well nurtured learns to mask and protect the *soul* in a thousand ways, to shore up the damage and avoid further threats of neglect or abuse.

Part of our job in counseling with adults whose *souls* have been wounded is to create safety, and to encourage the gentle uncovering of the armor that both protects them and keeps them stuck. In a supportive relationship, it is necessary to invite and challenge our clients to explore, to take the risk of leaving old patterns, and to discover new ways.

Here's a recent example from my own practice. Jim was facing a separation and divorce from his wife. He didn't choose it and he didn't want it. His anger, his hurt and feelings of betrayal all came forward in the confusion and sadness of his grieving. Loss of trust and erosion of respect had devastated the marriage. Jim's *soul* hungered for intimacy, for peace of mind, and for meaning out of the chaos. After a few weeks of counseling, he began to listen to the voices of his inner wisdom that were leading him to explore better options for coping. Because he was willing to engage in and trust his *soulful* deliberations, he emerged from his anguish, his sorrow, and his loss, as he discovered and claimed his autonomy more fully.

TENET II... *Our soul mediates all of our thoughts, feelings, choices and actions.*

Everything we experience impacts our *soul*, and everything we choose arises from our *soul*. Our *soul* has the job of interpreting, balancing and coping with all that we experience in our lives because we are whole human beings seeking balance. While perception starts out physiologically, it is instantly processed cognitively, affectively, and socially, as we consider all facets of our sense of who we are within our immediate culture and circumstances. *Soul* mediation is our inner wisdom trying to guide us toward our best opportunities and choices for survival and fulfillment. Coping well on a daily basis requires listening to our inner wisdom.

Examples of *soul* mediating physiology. Our bodies don't lie. Our story is told in our facial expressions, our posture, our tone of voice, our eye contact, and our overall vitality. It is common knowledge that many backaches, headaches and such result from stress and accompanying muscle tension. Just looking at some of the visceral figures of speech in our language, we can see the common validation of this knowledge.

Pain in the neck
My aching back!
I can't stomach this.

And just the opposite is true. In his book *Love and Survival: The Scientific Basis for the Healing Power of Intimacy*, physician and wholistic health advocate Dean Ornish (1998) provided a review of the evidence showing the important role of social support and intimacy in health and recovery from illness. He reports a Yale study of 119 men and forty women, all undergoing studies of blockages in coronary arteries, which found that, "Those who felt the most loved and supported had substantially less blockage in the arteries of their hearts." Similarly, it was found in a study of 131 women in Sweden, "that the availability of deep emotional relationships was associated with less coronary artery blockage as measured by computer-analyzed coronary angiography." In study after study, from many nations, of people of different ages and walks of life, the research supported the fact that intimate relationships improved overall health and recovery from illness or trauma. It is the love within these intimate relationships that nourishes our *souls*, and heals our bodies.

Of particular importance for counselors, psychotherapists, social workers, nurses, physicians and others in the health related professions is the knowledge gained in the landmark study in 1989 by David Spiegel and colleagues at Stanford Medical School. Ornish's review (1998, chapter two), reports:

> *In this study, women with metastatic breast cancer were randomly assigned to two groups. Both groups received conventional medical care such as chemotherapy, surgery, radiation and medications. In addition, one group of women met together for ninety minutes once-a-week for a year. Patients were encouraged to come regularly and to express their feelings about the illness and its effect on their lives in a supportive environment that felt safe enough for them to express what they were really feeling including their fears of disfigurement, of dying, of being abandoned by their friends and spouse, and so on.*

Ornish quotes Dr. Spiegel:

> *... the groups were structured to encourage discussion of how to cope with cancer, but at no time were patients led to believe that participation would affect the course of the disease.*

> *... social isolation was countered by developing strong relations among members... patients focused on how to extract meaning from tragedy by using their experience to help other patients and their families... clearly, the patients in these groups felt an intense bonding with one another and a sense of acceptance through sharing a common dilemma.*

Reporting on the outcome of Spiegel's study, Ornish writes: "These women who had the weekly support group lived an average of twice as long as did the other group of women who did not have the support group." In his summary he points out that, "Although the 'L' word (love) was not used in the journal report, as in most scientific publications, one could say that *these women began to love and care for each other*." (italics mine)

Research evidence is plentiful in detailing the effects of stress on bodies. Witmer and Sweeney (1992) report that as early as 1979, the United States Public Health Service "... found that at least 53 percent of the deaths in the United States are caused by life-style and self-destructive and negligent behavior."

Cognitions are mediated within our spiritual energy field. We are equipped with a host of variations of our cognitions, because survival favors such strength. All our cleverness is meant for coping.

> *The soul is the perceiver and revealer of truth.*
> — Ralph Waldo Emerson

Consider the complex subtle differences among the following.

Analyzing	Logical Sequential Thinking
Classifying	Monitoring
Diagnosing	Perceiving
Imagining	Problem solving

As counselors we need to remember that our clients, as well as we ourselves, are very complex beings. Cognitive psychologists have made an important contribution to our understanding of how internal self-talk may be distorted from previous wounds to the spirit. Negative self-talk will derail our best intentions to be well and whole. For example: "I can't do it!" is a belief system that sustains limitations. A counseling interaction to address this might be to suggest to the client that, "*It's not that you can't do it, it's that you won't do it. There is some choice here.*"

We know from the classic accounts of self-fulfilling prophecies by Rosenthal and Jacobson (1968), and on optimism by Seligman

(1990), that what we believe, or hold an image of, will tend to come true. Helping our clients to discover this level of awareness and to challenge distorted belief systems is an important contribution we can offer in attending to their *souls*. Witmer and Sweeney (1992) summarize this concept from Beck and Ellis:

> *Unhealthy persons who have mood disturbances are not emotionally sick, but cognitively wrong. That is, they are thinking irrational thoughts, doing faulty reasoning, or living by maladaptive rules made up of unrealistic or inappropriate 'shoulds' and 'oughts' or 'do's' and 'don'ts.' Research and clinical evidence have documented that negative thoughts that cause emotional turmoil nearly always contain gross distortions or unrealistic expectations.*

With all the distortions of our thoughts and beliefs from the expectations and injunctions of others, we must cope with the resulting stress and dysfunction that impacts our *soul*.

Emotions are mediated within our spiritual energy field. We commonly — and mistakenly — assume that we experience our feelings one at a time. In fact, we experience many feelings simultaneously (for example, sadness and relief, or anxiety and confusion). There is always an interplay that gets triggered among various feelings. A most vivid personal example is when I became aware that my anger was usually accompanied by hurt, fear, betrayal or disappointment. When my sweetheart left me, all these feelings combined with my frustration because things were happening to me that were out of my control.

Our emotions are a bit like strings on a musical instrument: as one string resonates, it triggers the vibration of another within the same family of chords. Even as a parent's voice resonates, a child might either be comforted or experience insult, depending on the intent of the parent.

This audible *soul* resonance might also explain how we can be differentially stimulated by music. Some music makes us want to dance, while other melodies or tempos may lead us to feel tranquil or reflective. Smells, like sounds, are powerful triggers for memories, stimulating images and flooding us with the feelings surrounding the remembered experience. All our emotional states are mediated from the spiritual center of our total being.

We all understand the expression *emotional turmoil*, but I think it is more appropriate to think of it as *spiritual turmoil*. If you are out of balance emotionally, it will manifest physically, cognitively and socially as well. We are not fragmented categorical beings. Our *soul* is our wholeness, and greater than the sum of our parts.

> ... *If every encounter with another is viewed as an opportunity to heal and extend love, one may learn to heal and be healed in relationship.*
>
> — Frances Vaughn

Social interaction is mediated by our spiritual field of awareness. Clearly we know that we must have bonds with other people if we are to be healthy. It is the connection to family, mate, friends, and community that helps to make us whole. It is from the love of others that we come to see ourselves as lovable and develop our capacity to return love. We need both to love and to be loved. Our quest is a longing to be intimate, to belong, and know intuitively that all nurturing, all healing, and all health are based in love from significant relationships.

Receiving this love is to be heard, to be seen, and to be embraced. We all need to tell our story and to be understood, accepted, appreciated, approved of, and validated as worthwhile human beings. It is within the context of caring relationships that we build intimacy, feel like we belong, build a sense of community, and find our sense of meaning and purpose.

> *The world is empty if one thinks only of mountains, rivers and cities, but to know someone here and there who thinks and feels with us, and who though distant, is close to us in spirit, this makes the earth for us an inhabited garden.*
>
> — Johann Wolfgang Goethe

When we are in authentic relationships, we are free to trust and express all of our thoughts, our attitudes, our values, and our moods. We become more transparent because it is safe to be our true selves. Intimate relationships invite us to respond with our whole being. Some people are graced with high-level social skills while others may struggle just trying to get comfortable with a few people. If you have been spiritually wounded by rejection, humiliation or other abuses in relationship with significant others, your ability to be intimate is severely compromised; your willingness to be open and caring is overshadowed by fear and mistrust.

Italian psychotherapist Roberto Assagioli (1965) suggested that "Spiritual refers not only to experiences considered religious but to all states of awareness, all the human functions and activities." Poetry, prayer, meditation, dance, music, play and athletic contests are but a few examples of the expression of the human spirit. Work, recreation, celebrations and rituals, laughter and humor, expressions of love and service to fellow humans are all essentially spiritual acts contributing to our well-being, within the loving bonds of our respective cultures.

Sherry is another former client who was sexually abused by her father as a child, a horrific and ultimate betrayal of trust. She was also rejected and neglected by her mother, and the consequence of this double insult to her *soul* left her sense of self dominated by doubt and shame. With such wounds to her spirit, she lost confidence in her ability to connect with others. Without these *soul* connecting bonds, she failed to build a sense of community, becoming more and more isolated. With years of counseling and medical support, her struggle has been very difficult, painful and courageous, with but slow gains.

As counselors and therapists, we need to recognize these deficiencies of love and loss of self-respect, and we need to prescribe more than behavioral and cognitive interventions. In *soul* counseling, we need to help our clients to find their way back, to reconnect to the great fabric of our culture of fellow humans.

TENET III... *Human life depends on love.*
We have known for certain, since the classic studies of René Spitz (Spitz & Cobliner, 1965), that children will die if they do not receive human touch. It is not just the touch; it is the voice tone,

the smile, the holding with gentle stroking, and the words of love which come from the parent or other significant caregiver. Without this continuing spiritual connection of love, humans will fail to develop their potential.

> *Love is the nature of the soul.*
> — John O'Donahue (1997)

In counseling, we have a very adequate vocabulary of spiritually meaningful words that could be subsumed under the heading "Expressions of Love." Here is a small sampling, from our common counseling lexicon, of terms which form the core of all relationships that promote growth and well-being.

Acceptance	Encouragement
Acknowledgment	Forgiveness
Caring	Gratitude
Commitment	Kindness
Compassion	Respect

These are all words of spiritual thought and action that are laden with potential for healing. They all involve meaningful relationships to others that arise from the core of our spirit, our humanness. They are all dimensions of love — the most tangible form of expression of our *soul*. We need to remember that *the relationship between love and well-being is causal, not coincidental.* The greater abundance of love in our lives, the healthier and happier we are. We need to integrate this message so thoroughly into our family and educational awareness at all levels that we know it as the foundation upon which everything else in our human development depends.

As caregivers, we know quite well the power inherent in the meaning and impact of love, as it is experienced — or not experienced — in our own lives as well as in the lives of our clients. Heidi Milardo, one of my former graduate students who served as a reader for an early draft of this manuscript, put it this way...

The most fulfilling experiences of our lives are founded in love for each other and for ourselves... I believe that my creativity, my pursuit of meaning in life through my role as mother, daughter, sister, wife, friend etc. and my 'new role' as a counselor all stem from my soul... I believe that not only do I give the gift of myself to my client, but I also receive the gift of knowing my client. Our souls do meet, we learn from each other, even 'love' each other, and I feel extremely fortunate about this.

Heidi closed with a quote from Joan Walsh Anglund (2001): "How shall we find love? It is ours in that instant we give it away."

The overall quality of one's relationships depends on how willing one is to be open, accepting, and loving rather than fearful, covert, and defensive.

— Frances Vaughn (1986)

Dean Ornish (1998) reports a follow-up survey of Harvard students from the 1950s, examining the relationships these students had with their parents. It was found that 91 percent of those who did not perceive themselves as having a warm relationship with their mothers had serious diseases diagnosed in midlife, compared with only 45 percent of those who perceived themselves to have had a warm relationship with their mothers. The researchers wrote, "The perception of love itself... may turn out to be a core biopsychosocial — spiritual buffer, reducing the negative impact of stressors and pathogens and promoting immune function and healing (p.34)." Survival favors love in every culture, in every class, at every age.

TENET IV... All life seeks to fulfill itself.

We need not to teach an acorn to grow into an oak tree, but when given a chance, it's intrinsic potentialities will develop. Similarly the human individual, given a chance, tends to develop his particular human potentialities... he will grow substantially undiverted, toward self-realization.

— Karen Horney (1956)

As humans, we are in a continuous process of evolving, becoming more aware, more conscious and more compassionate. This evolution occurs because survival favors those characteristics and behaviors in the long run. Our choices and decisions are made with primary consideration given to creating the best outcomes for the *self*. As our basic needs are met, and our spiritual awareness develops, our survival focus shifts, as Maslow (1970) so clearly showed us in his now-classic "Hierarchy of Needs." Our evolution is toward self-actualization. The same is true with plants; we see it in their foliage reaching for the sun and their roots driving ever more deeply in the soil in search of nourishment and water.

Carl Rogers (1980) put it this way:

> *We can say that there is in every organism, at whatever level, an underlying flow of movement toward constructive fulfillment of its inherent possibilities. In human beings, too, there is a natural tendency toward a more complex and complete development.* (pp. 117-118)

People who bring themselves to counseling in order to move toward self-actualization provide an example of the *soul* reaching for fulfillment. Those who seek counseling are at some level asking a question of supreme existential significance when they consider: "How can I make my life better?" Adler suggested that the purpose of the psychic life is to guarantee the continued experience on this earth of the human organism, and to enable each person to securely accomplish his or her own development. Witmer & Sweeney (1992) quote Maslow: "... self actualization and the pursuit toward health must now be accepted as a widespread and perhaps universal tendency (p. 128)."

This quest for meaning is the voice of our *soul* within. We are all seekers of a better life, one with meaning, satisfaction and fulfillment. It is in this spiritual arena that we seek and find balance and full functioning.

Many people have quite a lot of faith in themselves, particularly those we consider to be optimists and positive thinkers. In contrast, when people begin to doubt themselves, their judgment, their skills and their abilities to cope well in the world, their *soul* is telling them that all is not right. Clinical interpretations might use the diagnostic labels *depression* or *anxiety*, but it is much larger than this. There will be damage to their self-esteem if they have been set back by a job loss, a divorce, or other such wounds to the spirit. Some of these people will present themselves for counseling, and I believe that in our initial meetings, and perhaps throughout our time together, the most important thing I can give my clients is the gift of believing in them; that is to say, having faith in them. Hearing their *soul* stories, including their spiritual wounds of pain and despair, confusion, and sometimes their sense of hopelessness, tells me that they want things in their lives to be different. They come to me, trying to make things better.

I acknowledge that just the fact that they have brought themselves to counseling is a sign that something is trying to happen within them. The urge to grow and to transcend current dilemmas is present within them. I let them know that I have faith in the strength of their inner being. I see them questing for meaning, solace and fulfillment just as surely as all plant life seeks sunlight. Believing in my clients allows them to see themselves in a larger spectrum of possibility. It is never too late for clients to make better choices, and never too late for counselors to offer them encouragement as they strive for growth.

If support is not there in the lives of our clients, we have to help them find ways to create it and discover it. We must not let them stand alone, wobbling in the wind of chaos, if we can lend a hand for comfort, clarity and stability. All life wants to be balanced. As humans we strive to be spiritually centered. There is a constant drive for equilibrium as we move from existential angst...

... toward nurturing relationships
... toward peacefulness and satisfaction
... toward meaning and purpose
... toward fulfillment.

I believe it is safe to say that all people will thrive and flourish when they are in relationships where there is a spiritual connection of compassion.

❖ *A Gift from the Heart*

Not a strategy, technique or clever intervention
Not just intellectual
More than just emotional or social support
But a gift from the heart
How could counseling be anything but spiritual?

— dw

The implications of these four tenets for the helping professions are profound, because as counselors, social workers, psychologists, psychotherapists, physicians, nurses, and the full range of allied therapists, we have failed to fully honor the central themes of our basic humanness in much of our healing work. The evolution of our professional development has been limited by our science-only approach and our focus on the tangible exactitudes of details that can be measured. We need to broaden our perspective to include our intuitive human responses to the nuances of the *soul* of each client or patient — who is first of all a *person*. It is this spirit within each of us that is the essence of our being fully human.

Our work as counselors is to resonate deeply with the *souls* of our clients, in all their despair and all their potential.

A Beginning

It's a beginning
... a framework
a little like a model
   "T" Ford
lean and practical

May these ideas be useful
May they help bring us together
May they open new spheres
of connections and understanding
   with our clients

May they be a threshold
from which to move forward
to discover new dimensions of
   our humanness
and become more whole

I invite all who will join me
on this journey
Your challenges, and support
your ideas and the creative
   energy of your spirits

— dw

Soul Searching Journal Assignments — for Your Clients, and for Yourself

- Write your reaction and ideas about each of the four basic tenets, and how they might apply in your life.
- Reflect on how, in your own life, you are currently seeking to fulfill yourself. Ask yourself these questions: What do I need to do? What do I intend to do? What am I willing to do? When will I start? What will be my criteria for success?

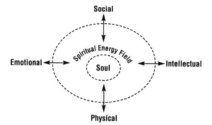

Social

Emotional ←→ Intellectual

Spiritual Energy Field

Soul

Physical

4

Counseling Process I
A Spiritual Framework

Clients arrive for counseling with a wide range of agendas. Some are seriously hurting from personal losses, failures, rejections, and other painful life experiences. Many are trying to improve or repair intimate relationships. Others are seeking to find themselves, to clarify their life goals, or to explore new directions. A few are just curious about what "counseling" might open up for them. Regardless of their reasons for seeking my help, there is a core of experiences I want for each client who comes to me.

❖ Ten Things I Want My Clients to Experience

1. Being WELCOMED. The first contact with my client is extremely important; I want to communicate safety and confidence in the initial encounter. I want to be ready for my client with an open mind and an open heart. My office is friendly. Forget the diplomas, certificates and licenses on the wall — I'll make that information available in a separate handout. One of the first jobs I have is to get down off of any pedestal — whether placed there by my client or by my own ego needs. I want to reduce the hierarchy so prevalent in our professional culture, and level the field on which we do our work. The warmth of my personal greeting and welcome will be revealed by my eye contact, tone of voice, handshake, spirit of sincere interest, and invitation to find a comfortable chair. My warmth of spirit will play a central part in creating a "safe" place. Since these expressions all come from within me, it is essential that I am centered and able to express caring and respect in spontaneous and natural ways. I want to reduce my clients' fear and anxiety, and create an atmosphere for them to explore their most personal thoughts and feelings.

It is important to communicate a genuine valuing to those who have shown the courage to bring themselves to counseling. Without the counselor's expressions of compassionate spirit, there will be no depth of rapport. The polarities of this presence, or lack of it, may be viewed in these specifics:

Soulful Orientation	Clinical Orientation
Attentive, present	Preoccupied with counselor's agenda
Warm, friendly	Aloof
Personal Connection	Objective, detached
Sees client as a person	Sees patient in terms of a diagnosis

If we think about what our clients may be experiencing prior to coming for counseling, they are no doubt wondering apprehensively...

What is wrong with me?
What is counseling going to be like?
What is my counselor going to be like?
Will this be someone I can <u>really</u> trust?
What am I supposed to do or say?
If I tell the counselor my secrets, what will s/he think of me?
Maybe I should just take care of my own issues?

The sooner you can demonstrate to the client that she will be treated with respect, and that the process doesn't have to be "clinical," the better your work together will go. A spirit of welcome at the first meeting can have a profound effect on the outcome.

If we can extend unconditional friendliness toward our own or another's whole range of experience and very being, this begins to penetrate the clouds of self-judgment, so our life energy can circulate freely again.
— John Welwood (2000)

From the outset, I want my clients to get a sense of what I believe is important about the counseling process because it will help them understand much more about our work together. No surprises, no hidden agendas, nothing supernatural. In our initial meeting, I give my clients an orientation packet for them to take home (see the appendix). I want to demystify the process.

2. *Being ACKNOWLEDGED.* As counselors, we might say something such as this:

I want to acknowledge that this is an important transition time in your life. While I don't yet know much about you, I know that your decision to seek help in sorting things out took courage and awareness that you want something positive to happen. Something new wants to emerge. I believe that coming for counseling arises out of wanting to understand yourself more fully and to find new paths, new ways of being. I want you to know that I will try to understand and I will honor your experiences as we work together.

The client's quest for change is significant. The counselor needs to *acknowledge* and to *validate* the importance of the issues presented, as well as the decision, and the courage it took to make it, in bringing himself to counseling. There are a number of personal qualities that emanate from the counselor's spirit, even in these early sessions. For example, you express *interest, acceptance, caring* and *respect*, all very spontaneously in response to what your clients are sharing with you about their lives. All these things continue to lay the groundwork for later challenges that you will offer within this supportive context.

3. *TRUST as the foundation of our work together.*

The healing power of unconditional love is no secret, but as long as one is afraid to trust, one can neither receive it nor offer it.

— Frances Vaughn (1986)

Trust allows the client to open the window to her *soul*, to reveal her true self. We can be open with others when we sense there is safety and compassion. Of course, the limits of confidentiality must be made clear and understood at the outset. These and other guidelines should be discussed and included in the information handout in the initial session.

The counselor's personal openness models trust and authenticity for clients. Are not trust and honesty the *soul* connection of genuine relationships?

> *Oh, the comfort, the inexpressible comfort of feeling safe with a person, having neither to weigh thoughts nor measure words, but pouring them all right out... just as they are chaff and grain together, certain that a faithful hand will take and sift them, keep what is worth keeping, and with the breath of kindness, blow the rest away.*
>
> — Anonymous Shoshone

4. POWER WITHIN THEMSELVES. I want clients to know that they have the power within themselves to create and choose the changes they want and that it is their responsibility. They need to know that they have the freedom to choose their belief systems, their attitudes and their behaviors. I invite them to work with me as collaborators, co-therapists and co-experimenters. The focus is on their power within, their freedom to choose, and their responsibility for manifesting the vitality of their *soul*. I like the way Carl Rogers (1980) put it:

> *Individuals have within themselves vast resources for self-understanding and for altering their self-concepts, basic attitudes, and self-directed behavior; these resources can be tapped if a climate of facilitative psychological attitudes can be provided.* (p. 115)

Too often, as counselors, we think of ourselves as empowering our clients, but we need to remember that the power is already within our clients. Our part is in helping them to discover and tap into their inner resources.

5. FACILITATION FOR PERSONAL GROWTH. I want clients to know that my job is to create the conditions that will help them move toward actualizing their potential:

I will listen to them and encourage them...

... to tell their story

... to face their fears

... to explore their hopes and dreams

... to make healthy choices

I will challenge them in supportive ways...

... to take risks in disclosing their truths

... to examine their resistance

... to look at how denial and other defenses work to protect them and also keep them stuck

... to make rebuttals to negative self-talk and counter-productive behavior

My primary purpose is to maximize opportunities for my clients to move toward growth in unfolding their unique potential.

*6. That I have **BELIEF AND FAITH IN THEM**.* I want clients to know early on that I believe in them, and have faith in their ability to transcend their current dilemmas and to develop in ways which will enrich their lives.

I'm convinced, from my own experience, that one of the greatest gifts I bring to my clients is my faith in them. It may just be a turning point for them to begin to have faith in themselves and to believe that they are good, worthwhile and deserving persons. It is this realignment of their beliefs about themselves that will allow them to claim their autonomy, and to see how this fundamental choice is essential for creating their own best circumstances.

John Welwood (2000) put it this way:

> *Orienting myself toward the basic goodness hidden beneath their conflicts and struggles, I could contact the deeper aliveness circulating within them and between the two of us in the present moment. This made possible a heart-connection that promoted real change.*

Later, he writes:

> *I found that if I could connect with the basic goodness in those I worked with — the underlying, often hidden longing and will to be who they are and meet life fully — not just as*

an ideal or as positive thinking, but as a living reality, then I could start to forge an alliance with the essential core of health within them.

7. FREEDOM FROM DIAGNOSIS, JUDGMENT AND CATEGORIES. As counselors, if we believe that our *souls* mediate all our attitudes, choices and behaviors, we need to reconceptualize how we think about our work. For example, as I hear my client Celeste tell her story, and she tells me that she can never feel good about herself again because she has been so devastated by betrayal, I do not think in terms of emotional depression, anxiety or any other such traditional diagnostic categories. I conceptualize her dilemma as her *soul* seeking to be healed from the wounds of being betrayed. I find myself wondering, "If Celeste sees herself as a victim, how can I help her through this grief in such a way that she begins to see things differently? How can I help her to connect to her *soul* strength within? How can I facilitate her gain of a new perspective of her life's opportunities and choices?" Diagnostic categories and judgments all place a degree of external control onto her, and to some extent, reduce her options. In contrast, I want to encourage her internal control and her own sense of possibilities.

8. COUNSELOR TRANSPARENCY. I want my clients to know where I am coming from. No hidden agenda is acceptable. Mystery is not a good tool for empowering clients. As a counselor concerned with *soul* matters, my wish is for my clients to become spiritually integrated. Their first steps along this path are to wake up and discover any counterproductive patterns in their choice-making and behavior. From a counseling theory perspective, this waking up and integration is closest to a Gestalt idea, because the focus on awareness is the foundation for building an undistorted sense of themselves. Awareness also helps clients connect to their own sense of authenticity, and to avoid masks and roles getting in the way.

To counsel in the *soul* arena is to use the contributions of all theoretical approaches. The principles of *person-centered theory* are most closely aligned with *soul* issues, as a compassionate and empathic counselor attempts to engage the inner self of the client.

These principles will set the tone, and help to create a safe environment. *Psychodynamic theory* will encourage exploration of the relevant historical perspective, and the impact of significant people and events in the client's early life. *Family systems thinking* will help us see the context of our clients' lives as we explore the relationships that continue to impact their lives in important ways. *Cognitive and behavioral approaches* will be helpful in challenging dysfunctional patterns and exploring new pathways. All these and other theories contribute because each provides a lens for exploring the context and *soul* fabric of our clients. They also provide a framework for understanding behavior and generating ideas for intervention strategies. Significant *soul* encounters are not the result of any technique or method, they are created by the person of the counselor that is able to integrate and use the existing theories in a broader *soul* framework. All these things should be transparent to our clients as we go about our work.

Soul counseling needs to be an integrative approach that attends to the hopes, dreams, as well as the spiritual wounds and dysfunctional patterns of the client.

9. CHALLENGE WITH SUPPORT. Counselors who move toward *soul* awareness in their work with clients need to be mindful of both challenge and support. We used to talk about confronting our clients' counterproductive patterns, but *challenge* is a much friendlier word than *confrontation.* I can challenge with caring and support, while confrontation suggests a more harsh and threatening tone, a sort of "I'm right and you're wrong" attitude. It's important that I challenge my clients to examine their counterproductive patterns if they are truly going to discover their pathways to possibilities. I want them to see what it is that they are doing that is keeping them from getting what they want.

> *There once was a man from Kartosis*
> *who had narrow perspective neurosis*
> *his attitudes you see*
> > *were as fixed as could be*
> > *and he died of psychosclerosis*
>
> — dw

Hardening of the Categories: Psychosclerosis. Old patterns of thought and behavior work for us and at the same time defeat us. We mistakenly think they keep us safe. Like old shoes, these patterns may be comfortable in their familiarity, but they don't always provide a solid foundation. They defeat us when they prevent us from challenging the rigidity and stuckness of our ways.

It is imperative, for our own well-being, that we remain flexible in our attitudes. Rigidity closes out options and clogs up the arteries of the imagination. Just as arterial sclerosis blocks oxygen to the heart or brain, *psychosclerosis* blocks new ideas and fresh perspectives in thinking, drawing the curtain of darkness ever more tightly against our view of the possibilities. It is the voice of our *souls* that we are stifling. We need to welcome the *soul* voice, wounds, warts and all.

> *The more defensive one is the more perception is distorted and the more one is subject to self-deception. Self-deception can be a major obstacle to healing, and almost everyone needs help from an outside observer, be it a therapist, teacher, or friend, in clearing it up. When one does not see oneself clearly, one cannot see others clearly, and one remains caught in a world of illusion where genuine presence and authentic contact with others is impossible.*
>
> — Frances Vaughn (1986)

Challenging Counterproductive Patterns. When I see behavior or patterns of behavior that I believe work against the best interests of my client, I owe it to my client to share my perceptions, thoughts and opinions. My challenge is meant to help the client to become more clear, as well as to expand my own understanding.

Some years ago, one of my clients disclosed that she was currently having sex with four different men. It was a dual role for the each of the men: one was her auto mechanic; another her butcher at the meat market; the third a carpenter she hired to do repairs; and still another, her gardener. All of them gave her a discount on their services or goods in return for sexual favors. I challenged her with something like the following:

> *"Joyce... what I am hearing is that you seem to be pleased with yourself in some respects because you are sleeping with four different men. Your car mechanic fixes your car; your carpenter fixes things around the house; your butcher provides you the best cuts of meat and then there is your gardener. I'm wondering if this behavior is in your best interest in the long run. I may be an old prude, but I find it difficult to believe that you feel good about yourself if you are bartering sex in return for favors? I'm imagining that you might have some doubts, but I'm not sure?"*

My intentions were to awaken Joyce to examine her motives, her choices, her actions and the long-term "big picture" perspective of the consequences of her behavior. Without challenge and examination, the status-quo rules. We do our clients a disservice when we fail to challenge. We implicitly condone, and are then complicit with, their counter-productive behavior.

In chapter seven of William Miller's book (1999), *Values, Spirituality and Psychotherapy*, Richards, Rector and Tjeltveit point out that confronting clients regarding unhealthy values may threaten the therapeutic relationship. This is because in our culture, we are conditioned to be "nice," and not to hurt anyone's feelings. While most counselors want to be "nice people," we must not get caught up in failing to challenge our clients' dysfunctional behavior. The line between challenging an issue and letting it go can be illusive. After all, aren't we vigilant in our efforts to avoid being judgmental? It is a fine line, and will be different with each client. But the counselor must be free to give honest constructive feedback to clients; it has to be part of the understanding and agreement of the relationship. If we are not, if we're too hesitant or passive, we get caught up in our clients' protective armor, and we support them in remaining stuck. This is not unlike the co-dependent person in relationship with a manipulative partner.

The Respect of Being Tentative. Our challenges must be tentative as we share our observations and perceptions of what is going on regarding the behaviors and patterns we see as dysfunctional. The last thing my client needs is to feel exposed by some "know it all" who simply advises and moralizes. In sharing my observations, I need to show respect for their struggles and their desire to transcend them. I need to be transparent and to let my clients know where I am coming from. It is a delicate thing to challenge our clients, without causing them to feel threatened. It must be a gentle musing: *"I wonder if...,"* or *"I suspect that..."* It is an invitation for them to consider letting go of this pattern if they see it as counterproductive.

We can only speculate; we do not have absolute knowledge. If the counselor's comments are overly authoritative, they are presumptuous, and run the risk of stifling the client's growth or creating an unwanted dependency. Our job is to empower our clients, and being tentative shows respectful humility, as we ask, "I wonder if this could be the situation here, I'm not sure...?" Such uncertainty is honest and particularly appropriate when we are in a relationship with a person from a different culture (which, when viewed from the multitude of sub-cultural perspectives, is almost everyone). When we consider differences of ethnic origin, religion, age, gender, sexual orientation, education, socioeconomic background, family environment, and other variables, we can only speculate on the meaning that these experiences have for our client. There are very real sub-cultural differences impacting each of our clients. Responding tentatively, and with respect for the client's own inner knowing, builds a deeper level of rapport, allowing the clients to begin to see that we accept them, and to come to believe that we may even understand some of the puzzle. Discovering their own inner knowing is enormously empowering; they may begin to look for their locus of authority within themselves instead of in their outer world of perceived external experts.

Still, challenge is our most difficult intervention, because it is the most threatening to our clients. We need to present challenge in the context of support and encouragement. If we avoid challenges, and let our clients off the hook, we are caught in our own co-dependence. It could be likened unto a person enabling her alcoholic partner, saying, *"It's okay, things will be better tomorrow."* The meta-message here is, *"Just don't leave me."*

10. RELIANCE UPON THEIR OWN SOUL IN PERSONAL DECISIONS. At some point in the counseling process I will need to broach the idea of *soul*, in such a way that it is acceptable and not in conflict with the client's religious or other spiritual beliefs. There has been a certain taboo in our counseling culture with regard to bringing up religious or spiritual matters. Rightfully so, in many respects. The fear is that clients will be proselytized or otherwise manipulated by their counselors. The boundary is, *"No solicitation, please."* We value our individual right to choose. Any inquiry into another person's religious and/or spiritual issues must (like any other challenge) be done very tentatively and with great respect. The question arises: *How does the counselor broach the issue of spiritual life?*

I prefer to invite my clients' thoughts on their spiritual beliefs and experiences in their lives with the initial take-home questionnaire and autobiographical assignment (see the appendix). This provides a point of reference for future inquiry and discussion. Richards, Rector and Tjeltveit (1999) take a more direct approach:

> *Therapists can facilitate the integration of spirituality into treatment by asking clients whether they can think of ways that their spiritual beliefs and values might help them cope with their problems. By helping clients affirm their core spiritual values, live congruently with these values, and access the spiritual resources of their lives (i.e., their spiritual beliefs, values, practices and community), therapists can more effectively assist clients in their efforts to cope, heal, and grow.* (p. 156).

I think such inquiry is fine as long as we are not pushing an agenda or a particular viewpoint. It is very important that we not impose our spiritual and religious values or points of view on our clients, but if our perspective is such that we determine their beliefs on these issues are causing them or others harm, it is imperative that we challenge what we observe as dysfunctional patterns.

These ten experiential elements of the process are important themes that permeate my counseling work. They are not lock-step or cookie-cutter crisp, nor are they an exhaustive and complete list of the complex dynamics in the counseling process. There is no exact sequence; there is much overlap among these elements; and there are many other matters counselors must consider.

I want my clients to know that I don't always have an answer for them and I don't always know what to say in every instance. This kind of transparency and congruence will add to the trust of the therapeutic exchange. I like what Carl Jung (1933) wrote in this regard:

> *It must be a relief to every serious-minded person to hear that the psychologist also does not always know what to say. Such a confession is often the beginning of the patient's confidence in him.* (p. 336).

❖ Teaching Our Clients

> *Nothing positive can happen in our lives unless we are willing.*
> — Anne Wilson Schaef (1999)

I noticed a few years ago in my university teaching that the personal growth of my students was emerging more quickly and more abundantly than it was with my clients. The facetious conclusion I came to was that I should refer all my clients to our graduate program in counseling.

That there should be such personal growth in our students is no surprise, since they come to us more aware and more willing. In a sense, we all enter into the helping professions eager to learn more about ourselves and to understand some unresolved issues in our own lives as well as the lives of others. As our students learn the core theoretical and knowledge bases in the psychology of human behavior, they also have the opportunity to work on their own personal development in a group counseling laboratory experience and other seminars with experiential components. I believe this personal growth work is of utmost importance as the foundational piece of their professional education! What could be more important in the helping professions than to have whole and aware persons serving clients?

But since the vast majority of my clients will not enter our counselor education program, I want to provide them with at least a modicum of tutoring on how their lives have unfolded, and to invite them to consider what they might do to be more aware and more personally responsible for making desirable changes.

I am reluctant to admit that teaching could be an important piece of learning within the counseling context. I resist being pedantic. At the same time, I want my clients to move as quickly as possible toward greater self-awareness, if my instructional reflections and challenges can be received well. Teaching goes on advertently or inadvertently in any event, by what we say and what we do. Over the years, I have erred in the direction of *"not pushing instruction,"* but I'm getting a little more liberated from my somewhat blind loyalty to my own self-imposed limitations on how I interpreted person-centered theory. When I came to more fully understand Rogers's ideas of congruence, authenticity and transparency, I realized I had great freedom to be myself, which I have come to believe is exactly what Rogers intended. If my clients can make sense of my observations and not feel threatened, they can become more active as collaborators. As part of my teaching, I think it is a good idea to take a few minutes at the end of each session to debrief important learnings that come up for my clients.

Twelve Levels of Awareness for Clients to Learn in Counseling

Without awareness of possibilities, there are no choices. Here are twelve things I would like my clients to consider and come to believe in, if by chance and circumstance they have not yet come to understand on their own.

1. I have a soul, an inner consciousness that wants me to be well and happy, and to fulfill myself.

2. My inner self is my most dependable choice maker.

3. I have the freedom to choose my thoughts, feelings, attitudes, beliefs and behaviors in any given set of circumstances.

4. I can learn to recognize my feelings at the time I am experiencing them.

5. I can learn by examining my attitudes about my own experiences and my view of the world. For example: Am I positive and optimistic, or negative and pessimistic? Can I learn how my attitudes might have been formed? (E.g., parental injunctions; peer norms and expectations; personal awareness; choices that have been positively reinforced.)

6. I can catch myself in any self-discounting. Humility is one thing, but being self-effacing with subtle put-downs or not-so-subtle personal self-insults will undermine my self-esteem and my integrity.

7. I will not allow others to put me down in any way. I will be open to compassionate challenge, but I will not take insult on board. It is toxic, I don't need it, and I don't want it.

8. I can recognize my cognitive distortions. Some examples: overgeneralization; black-and-white thinking; jumping to conclusions; exaggerating or minimizing; "should" statements; disqualifying the positive.

9. I can make a rebuttal to negativity. It is important to challenge any negative energy coming from external sources, as well as my own negative self-talk. Unchallenged, this negativity becomes an entrenched belief about myself. For example:

Negative Self-Talk	Affirming Self-Talk
I can't do it!	*I can try, and I will.*
I don't know how!	*I'll learn!*
What if I make a mistake?	*I will learn from it.*

Negative self-talk keeps people from going forward, and counselors need to discourage negative self-fulfilling prophecies. I often invite clients to try out new belief systems. For example: They may say, *"I could never do that."* If they hold on to this belief, it will be part of their unconscious "hard disk" memory. I ask that they simply put that negative attitude in the past tense and then try out a new attitude that says, *"I didn't used to be able to do this, and I'm choosing to learn to do it now and will put myself to the task."* It's a way of reframing the sense of self, and taking things out of rigid categories.

It is important to point out *self-talk* to clients. I find that if they more clearly understand their internal struggles, they can give expression to the various voices that want to be heard. Clients often have overly active *should* voices. They also have polarized voices that are simultaneously hopeful and discouraged, self-doubting and optimistic, angry and loving, mixtures of all these, and more.

10. I can listen to my pain, and learn from my symptoms. Symptoms hold the key to solutions. Gestalt guru Fritz Perls (1969) might have said, "Give your symptoms a voice. What would they say to you?" If, for example, I am angry, and ask my anger what it wants to tell me, I might hear: *"I am angry because I have been hurt, and I am afraid to admit it."* I then need to listen and to see the hurt that accompanies my anger, and attempt to understand why I am afraid to make myself vulnerable by admitting my hurt. All of our symptoms are signals from our wounds, and as such will hold a key to our self-understanding. I invite my clients to learn what they can from their symptoms, and to discover what they need to do to get through their own painful passage. If they will listen to the inner voice of their *soul*, they will know.

11. I can recall my childhood innocence and claim my essential goodness.

12. I can create a plan for change and then commit to it. For example:

- to be willing to suspend old belief systems.
- to take responsibility to experiment with new attitudes.
- to take on assignments, give myself new challenges, and make a commitment to change.
- to try out new behaviors that are positive for my development.

Counselors may serve in some ways as coaches, collaborating with clients in designing assignments for personal growth. Assignments are important because it takes practice to break old patterns and create new ways with more desirable outcomes. As clients begin to experience success in their choices and new directions, the tangible evidence of their progress will be very encouraging and will reinforce their continuing effort. Each gain should be acknowledged to further reinforce their positive movement.

It is worth noting, as you reflect upon the material in this chapter, that counseling of any kind can't be reduced to ten of this and twelve of that. Nevertheless, the essentials can be highlighted. I believe you will find this framework useful as you consider the possibility of adding a *soul* dimension to your counseling practice.

Soul Searching Journal Assignments — for Your Clients, and for Yourself

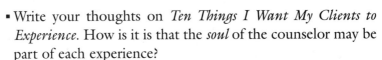

- Write your thoughts on *Ten Things I Want My Clients to Experience*. How is it is that the *soul* of the counselor may be part of each experience?
- Comment on your reactions to each of the *Twelve Levels of Awareness for Clients to Learn in Counseling*.

5

Counseling Process II
Attending to Matters of the Soul

Presence is the soul texture of a person.
— John O'Donahue

In chapter 4, our focus was on the foundations of counseling, with emphasis on connecting with the *soul* of the client. In this chapter, we're going to look at some specific counselor behaviors that will help you to respond more effectively to the *soul* wounds of your clients.

❖ *Being Fully Present*

John Welwood (2000) captures the essence of this concept when he writes:

> *Before we can truly embody this vast space of empathy and compassion for others, where we can totally let them be who they are, we must first be on friendly terms with our own raw and tender feelings. For many of us this may be the hardest path of all — opening our hearts to ourselves.* (p.31)

As professionals, we will have spiritual turmoil on occasion, as we suffer loss or setbacks, disappointments and difficult circumstances, but we are obliged to deal with these effectively and to come to our *soul* work in counseling with a clean slate. The *tone* that we bring to our work should be peaceful and stable. We should be centered and aware of our own issues. A counselor without this clarity is impaired. When you're distracted with your own concerns, you cannot listen well. This will be manifest in your body language and your inability to focus, and your client will sense it.

If you are with a person who is sad and agitated by frustration, you feel and resonate with their dispirited state, just as you do with another who is joyous, peaceful and contented. If we are truly present in the moment, we are not immune to the spiritual energy that flows between our clients and ourselves, and we become aware of a spiritual synchronicity that develops between two people when there is close resonance and empathy.

I am reminded of a story that Carl Rogers (1980) told about going into session with a client just after being informed by his secretary that his wife had been in a car accident. Although his wife was apparently okay, she had been checked into the hospital for examination. After just a few minutes, Rogers became aware of his nagging distraction and, knowing that he needed to interrupt the session, he said something like, "I'm sorry but I'm not very able to be present with you right now. My secretary just mentioned that my wife was in the hospital, and I'm distracted. I need to make a telephone call to clarify this." His client said, "Phew! I thought it was me!" *Isn't it interesting that the client was picking up signals of distraction, but like so many clients who may be deferential to authority, he blamed himself.* Rogers knew that he needed to clear his concerns before he could truly hear and engage the spirit of his client. His solution was simply to be congruent and transparent, admitting his distraction, and then taking care of it immediately. Better to interrupt the session for five minutes than to "fake it" for fifty minutes. As it turned out, his wife was not in serious condition and, being reassured, Rogers was able to return and be fully present with his client.

Before I can begin to connect to and engage the *soul* of my client, I must be as unburdened as possible by any of my own personal spiritual turmoil. When my client arrives at my door, I want to be receptive, open, fully present, and at peace. As counselors, we need to attain a level of personal spiritual growth that will give us clarity to be more fully present in the moment.

The old adage, *"I can't take my client any further down the path than I have traveled,"* advises us well here.

Three Levels of Counselor Awareness

Level One: Sensory Awareness. Examples of a counselor's private thoughts: "I'm thirsty." "What's the weather doing?" "I need to get some exercise." "Here comes my client; she looks a little weary."

At this level, our minds are free-wheeling; we are unfocused. Any stimulus can distract us. Daydreaming is common. Boredom or fatigue can take us to this level. It is the domain of random and inappropriate thoughts. This is a private (not transparent) world of inner thoughts, and sensations. This level closes when we enter level two.

Level Two: Being Present in the Moment. Examples of a counselor's private thoughts: "This woman entering my office seems to be in distress. Her facial expression and body posture suggest tension and sadness. I wonder how I can help."

On this level the counselor is transitioning and becoming more focused, paying more attention to details, observing, listening carefully, and making non-judgmental assessments. We shift from our private thoughts to being more transparent; our authenticity as counselors requires us to be more open with how we are experiencing our clients. These are the beginning resonances of *soul* connection with the client.

Level Three: *Soul* Awareness. Examples of a counselor's private thoughts: "I want her to know that I accept her as she is, and that I think I understand, a least a little bit. I want her to experience my caring for her and my desire to help. From my transparency, she will know that I respect her and feel these things from what I say, the tone of my voice, my eye contact, and my body posture."

At this level, we are beginning to get some feeling of *soul* connections. We are getting a solid feeling for the ground we stand on with the client. Our responses will demonstrate compassion that will include challenge as well as support, along with encouragement for making healthy choices. It is a time of being fully present and making a *soul* connection with the client.

❖ *Hearing the Story*

When we listen to another person with genuine interest and presence, we open ourselves to the inner core experience of the other. When I can truly catch the spirit of my client, I feel a deep connection to the wholeness of her being, and her message becomes more clear.

Monica, one of my students, wrote the following in her journal:

It was at the age of fourteen that I saw my first counselor. From the moment I opened my mouth I could not stop spilling out my story. Finally, I thought, someone who will genuinely listen and demonstrate some level of caring, even if being paid to do so! It was quite validating and brought such freedom in that I was able to release my emotional burdens. Two years later I met Desiree, an African American woman who saw me in her home and baked the most delicious cakes and brewed the best cappuccino I have ever tasted. Her little home was quite rustic yet warm and inviting. Talking and sharing with her was the most therapeutic for me of all the counselors I saw during my adolescent years. Through her guidance I was able to develop the most confidence in myself as well as the desire for meaning in my life. I felt truly empowered for the first time — to love myself for who I am, to achieve greater things and to not settle for less in any aspect of my life. Those sessions were so rich and meaningful, and not simply because of the gourmet cakes! I savored every moment with Desiree. She believed in me! I believe she helped to save my soul, for when we met I was experiencing what I believe was clinical depression and wanted to die to relieve myself of the aching sadness within.

As each of our clients' stories unfolds, we hear their sorrow, their pain, their fear and their frustration; we hear their hopes and their dreams. As we begin to understand their multi-layered context, we get a glimpse of how it may be that they are stuck. For example, we all know people whose spirits are dampened and expressed in very passive ways, and others whose frenetic and manic-like behavior reveals their distress. If we listen to their stories, we will come to see how these patterns originated, why they pay off, and why they repeat themselves. We all know from Psych 101 that *behavior that gets reinforced gets repeated*. Because of this reinforcement and repetition, patterns get very well established, even entrenched.

> *A psychoneurosis must be understood, ultimately, as the suffering of the soul which has not discovered its meaning.*
> — Carl Jung (1933)

❖ Intuition and Spontaneity

> *Intuition is our highest form of intelligence*
> — J. Krishnamurti (1953)

I was significantly impacted when I read these words by Krishnamurti; they rang so true for me. This kind of learning is an "Aha!" experience — when we realize that we already knew something to be true, but didn't know we knew it! Intuition is a voice of inner wisdom. It is our *soul* sensing, and includes cognition, perception, experience, emotion, memory and common sense. All of these many factors and others are mediated by the *soul* as we come to a more complete sensing of our options.

Some years ago, I initiated a program in the elementary schools in Portsmouth, New Hampshire that brought parents and grandparents as paraprofessionals into classrooms to work with young people who were not doing well with their peers and in their personal and social development in school. At a staff meeting early in the first year, Melissa Costa, a paraprofessional working in the second grade asked: *"What should I do with Jimmy? He hides in the classroom closet or in the bookshelves and refuses to participate in any classroom learning activities. I don't know what to do."* I said, *"I don't know either. What does your intuition tell you to do? What are your instincts here?"* I was quite aware that in a professional workplace, the protocol is to "ask the expert." He is the director (fancy title), and has a Ph.D. (supposed to know everything). In our culture, there are implicit hierarchies of expertise, which tell paraprofessionals that they should look to administrators and other professionals for guidance. If I fall into this trap, playing my professional role as the "expert" in this cultural expectation, I would be phony and pretend to know the absolute final word, perhaps saying something like, *"When seven-year-old boys hide in bookshelves or closets, do 'X', 'Y' and, of course, 'Z'."* Such rigid "expert" responses, in addition to being a pretense, do not allow for an open forum of idea sharing. It is a trap into which I wasn't then — and am not now — willing to fall.

The truth is that there are no exact answers to these questions in any text, nor is there research evidence that speaks with absolute authority on these matters. We don't always know for certain just what to do. So I answered: *"Melissa, I trust you. You were selected for this work because you have had success with kids, and you have a loving heart, and a good philosophy of what makes for healthy children. Just do what you think is right for Jimmy. Follow your intuition."*

At the staff meeting next week she said: *"I don't know if it's right, or if you're going to like it, but here is what happened: Jimmy was hiding out in the bookshelves and didn't want to come out. So, I picked him up, and carried him over to the reading lesson, and just sat holding him in my lap. For the first few minutes, Jimmy was as stiff as a board, but then I just felt him relax in my arms. After a few minutes, I didn't have to restrain him, and he sat comfortably on my lap. The next day, he was hiding out, and I just offered my hand and he came with me to the lesson, sitting at my feet with my hands on his shoulders. On the third day, he came looking for me!"*

This has to be one of the most astonishing stories of the power of humanness, of spiritual connection, of love in action, that I have witnessed in more than forty years of work in education. Here was Jimmy, this seven-year-old boy from a severely dysfunctional family, who was in danger of being institutionalized — at that time (1972) they did not have the federal legislation in place to provide for his special needs. With Melissa as a very loving, caring and consistent surrogate mother, Jimmy began to participate in school lessons, to cooperate and to play well with others on the playground. I believe she saved his life! Certainly she turned it around in a significant way. No amount of graduate training or advanced degrees or expertise in theoretical applications could have guided an intervention as well because these experiences are often too cooked in the cake of cognitive custom and the limitations of science. The *heart* of the matter is too often overlooked.

Another example of a brilliant trusting of intuition may be seen in the work of one of my students, Pat Wilsczynski. When Pat learned what we were doing in the Portsmouth Schools, she wanted to be involved, and signed up for an independent study project. She assigned herself to Sarah, a second grade student, who was new to the school. It was October, and in the five weeks that Sarah had been in school, she had not interacted significantly with anyone. Indeed, she rarely spoke, and when she did, it was just a whisper. Sarah did her work in class, but was socially isolated from her peers and her adult caregivers. Pat knew intuitively that the most important thing she could do would be just to sit with Sarah at her desk, reading a book or writing a story with her, or helping her with any other school tasks; in short, to be a friend. In just a few days, Sarah knew that she had a friend and her face would light up whenever Pat came in the room. Something spiritual was happening. There were no clever behavioral assignments, there was just this quiet acceptance with no pressure to do anything differently. There was no value judgment about Sarah's quiet isolation, just a genuine interest and caring. Within a week or two, you could visibly see that Sarah was a happier girl. She began to relate with her peers, first on the playground and later in the classroom. By March, Sarah had the lead in the class play!

What is this transformational experience all about? Pat did not concern herself with a specified plan. Rather, she had faith in Sarah and in her own global kind of hoping and sensing that Sarah would come out of her shell if she just got validating love for who she is. It was Pat's spirit expressed in an intuitively compassionate way. It was the special love that a mother has for her child — a bonding. Sarah experienced being cared about, being hoped about, and feeling that Pat liked her and had confidence in her. This gave Sarah the strength to emerge. Pat later took her masters degree in counseling and has had a very successful career in counseling for the past thirty years. She has also had a successful life as a wife, a mom, and a friend. Her competencies have much to do with her compassion and her intuition.

Even though intuition and spontaneity do not reveal observable logical deliberation, and in that sense seem to lack elements of scientific predictability, there is a confident inner knowing which, while it may seem mysterious, is based more in what Carl Rogers called "organismic sensing." In this regard, Rogers (1980) wrote:

> *I am compelled to believe that I, like many others, have underestimated the importance of this mystical spiritual dimension... I find that when I am closest to my inner, intuitive self, when I am somehow in touch with the unknown in me, when perhaps I am in a slightly altered state of consciousness, then whatever I do seems to be full of healing. Then simply my presence is releasing and helpful to the other.* (pp. 129-130)

❖ *Transparency, Congruence and Appropriate Self-disclosure*

> *The attitude of the psychotherapist is infinitely more important than the theories and methods of psychotherapy, that is why I was particularly concerned to make this attitude known.*
>
> — Carl Jung

Brian Thorne (1998) offers a transparency challenge to therapists:

> *When you are next stuck in your work with a client, acknowledge your stuckness and invite your client to join you in waiting without anxiety for the process to unfold. If you genuinely care for your client and he or she knows that you care, you may well be astonished by what follows. You will also know something about what many of your colleagues call spirituality even if you choose never to employ the word.* (p. 79-80)

While it is not usually appropriate for counselors to discuss their own spiritual or religious values and beliefs, particularly with minors or in domains in which separation of church and state are important, we should not restrict our natural warmth when expressing spiritual *values*, such as respect and compassion.

I want my clients to sense my optimism that the world presents opportunities and that we all have choices. I want to be spontaneous and congruent, in these and other matters, about who I am and what I value. While this models openness, it may also be threatening for a client who may feel she can never live up to such a way of being. I learned from one client that my optimism and high expectations put her at risk to experience discouragement and shame if she should disappoint me. While I need to be aware of this, I am still willing to allow my clients, and in a sense everyone I know, to have an impression of who I am, what I stand for, and how committed or passionate I am to my life's chosen ways. All these things are reasonably evident in all of us, if we are willing to be transparent as they are a direct reflection of our *soul* state of being.

> *Healing occurs when one is willing to risk being and expressing all that one is in relationship.*
> — Frances Vaughn (1986)

Sometimes we will be on personally familiar ground as we listen to a client's story. We may have experienced something similar. To let the client know this may be helpful because it demonstrates that...

... you probably can understand
... you won't be judgmental
... there will be less hierarchical distance as your client sees you as a person, and not just an authority figure
... there will be a bond of common ground on which to bridge understanding.

For example, I didn't have to tell Jim that I had been divorced earlier because he knew it from my book, *50 Ways to Love Your*

Leaver. He searched me out on the Internet and asked if he could work with me because my book was resonating deeply with him in his current state, grieving the loss of his marriage. With this common experience being known, it gave him trust and confidence in me, and gave me an opportunity to share more openly as I saw parallels in his experience of dealing with loss.

For me, the three rules of thumb about self-disclosure are to be aware of *(1) my motives for disclosing, (2) whose needs are being met,* and *(3) how might my disclosure be helpful.*

Boundaries, Dependency and Other Ethical Considerations

Soul counseling, by the depth of its connection, will create a bond between counselor and client. Cheryl, one of my graduate students, told the following very human story about "Becky," her counselee at a summer camp.

> *Becky was a foster child and upon meeting her, she appeared to be the most sad seven-year-old little girl I had ever seen. She was sullen, withdrawn, and never smiled. She also seemed quite fearful and suspicious toward one of the male counselors. I had enormous compassion for her and reached out gently as a friend to spend time with her. In just a few days, we were pals and her face and eyes brightened with her smile. A few days later, Becky even chose to do a special activity with the male counselor that she had shown such a strong negative reaction to earlier. By the end of the summer camp, she was one of the most active and popular girls in camp. She was even calling me "Mommy." I miss her and would love to see her again, but I am hesitant... When her foster mother failed to pick her up at the end of camp, I had fantasies of wanting to adopt her. I probably would have tried if I'd been old enough.*

This story touched all of us, and I thought "transference" just doesn't do justice to explaining the depth of connection and the observable growth of spirit that Becky exhibited as a result of

Cheryl's compassion. It seems plausible that Cheryl might very well have been a very good choice for becoming an adoptive mother for Becky. While Cheryl realized this couldn't be, her bond with Becky was understandable, and would, by anyone's standard, be judged as helpful. As to a follow-up letter or even a visit, I see no harm in this. But the ethical question of boundaries may be raised in this case, and in any case in which the counselor's equilibrium is tilted toward continuing the relationship beyond the parameters of their professional contact. When there is such deep heart-felt spiritual connection with another person, there will be a sense of loss at the ending of that relationship. Certainly supervision and personal counseling for the counselor would be appropriate support in such cases.

These deep feelings are not wrong, they are in fact the connecting tissue for the healing energies that are released because of the counselor's heartfelt caring. We need to be mindful of the standards that require us to be very clear in bringing no harm to our clients. It behooves us to continually examine our motives and our needs as counselors. Our first question to ourselves should be: *"Whose needs are being met?"* The following questions should be: *"What are the consequences for my client?"* *"Will I create a dependency?"* and so on. We will have to let go of many clients that we have cared for deeply, and it will help if we remind ourselves that our connection has made a contribution to their lives. Some clients will want to stay in touch, and counselors will want to keep in touch with some clients. These will be individual decisions, with counselors always keeping in focus the goal of *"What is best for my client?"*

It is well known, understood and accepted that Carl Rogers stayed in touch with "Gloria" who was so briefly his client in the film series entitled: *Three Approaches to Psychotherapy.* They formed a bond and a friendship, keeping in touch through correspondence for a number of years.

Much has been said in the human services professions in recent years about the ethics of "dual relationships." While it is universally agreed that any sexual relationship with a client or ex-client is unethical, other connections are not as clear. Readers are encouraged to consult the ethical guidelines of their professional societies, and recent discussions in the literature. I particularly like *Issues and Ethics in the Helping Professions* by Corey, Corey and Callanan (2003). In their introductory chapter, they acknowledge that while professional codes of ethics are essential, "The challenge comes with learning how to think critically and knowing ways to apply general ethical principles to particular situations." (p. 30)

❖ *Advantages and Disadvantages of Goal Setting*

There may be inherent dangers in setting specific goals with clients. For example, clients may hide other more important issues as they please us with their progress reports on their stated goals. In that sense, goals can serve as a smoke-screen form of resistance. Another shortfall of goals is that they often require specific and sustained focus that can lead to tunnel vision. Such blinders discourage peripheral perspective. We should not be too quick in trying to get our clients to set goals. Certainly we want to get as broad and as deep an understanding as we can about their history, their current context and future visions before directional paths are encouraged. One of the positive things about having goals is that it may bring focus and sequential benchmarks to our work.

Because my philosophy is not to push my agenda, and because of the dangers of hiding behind goals and the tunnel vision of a singular goal, I prefer to let goals emerge from my client as our work together evolves. If I am *in tune* with my client, and hearing subtle and not-so-subtle hints about the edges of growth toward which she is reaching, I simply observe this as a *possible* goal, and let her clarify and confirm or negate that observation. If my client confirms a desirable direction in which she wants to move (for example, away from toxic relationships or counter-productive behaviors, or toward a positive objective — such as to lose excess weight or quit smoking), I support this.

I also encourage my clients to identify their own resistance to getting what they say they want. We are all creatures of habit. We unconsciously repeat our "old ways" because they are known, or they have in some way worked in the past and we get in a groove.

While these patterns may be comfortable, like old shoes, such comfort may lead us to succumb to another of Newton's laws: *Bodies at rest tend to remain at rest.* Being stuck in old patterns is one way clients sabotage their efforts to change. When my clients are "fed-up" and sick of the way things are for them (sometimes literally sick), an opportunity is created to challenge them in a supportive and caring way. I might invite them to create a list of specific things that they could do to change counter-productive patterns. For example:

- Don't allow put downs from others
- Move away from relationships that are not healthy for you
- Challenge self-doubts
- Avoid self-put-downs
- Catch yourself in negative self-talk and offer a rebuttal.

Goals need to be co-created with our clients. They should be attainable, and designed in small increments for success. The question of commitment and self-discipline to stay on task will be a continuing challenge in our work. Only the client's *soul* as choice-maker can muster the self-discipline for commitment. *Willpower will be driven by a clear soul message of intention and expectation.*

I see my work as helping clients to create a context of hope in their search for clarity, peace and purpose. It is my intention to challenge my clients to examine the behaviors and attitudes that are not serving them, and encourage them toward making choices that will create new positive experiences.

Giving Assignments

It is typical for clients to attend counseling one hour a week. Given this short amount of work time, I think it's is useful to engage clients in relevant personal growth assignments for at least part of the 167 hours they have till the next time they see me. The first assignment is given on the first visit, when I invite them to respond to autobiographical reflections, perspectives and considerations (see the Appendix). Two others I may use are described briefly below.

Journaling. Just as I encourage readers to engage in *soul-*searching journal entries for each chapter in this book, I also encourage my clients to keep loose-leaf journals throughout their work with me. They are free to share as much or as little of their journal with me as they wish. Journals provide an important avenue for expressing inner thoughts and feelings. As we make our journal entries, we know intuitively that we must write the truth. For example: *If I am hiding from the truth in my life, then I must write about that truth-hiding in my journal.* Journaling is a way to chart progress toward our stated goals, a way to challenge ourselves and to listen to all the voices wanting *"air time"* in our heads. Each journal entry can open a frontier for us to enter into our spiritual quest for becoming what we can imagine for ourselves. Journaling supports our work by inviting clients to explore important spiritual questions in their lives.

Behavioral Assignments. If I am working with a person who is shy and wanting to become more social and able to assert himself more effectively, the most natural thing in the world is to work out some ideas together for "real-life behaviors" that he would be willing to try. We know from the cognitive and behavioral theories that these efforts should be small steps, starting with behaviors that can be successful. Each step met with success reinforces the desired behavior. Practice, practice, and more practice will bring us to our goal. Naturally there needs to be accompanying engagement of the *soul* in the process of supporting these activities.

Dan and His Bicycle: A story of encouragement and participatory action

Sometimes my intuition tells me it is appropriate to get directly involved in helping a client to initiate a new behavior. This is especially true for certain children and adolescents, particularly if they are lacking in confidence and afraid to try new things.

Dan was an eighth-grader who didn't know how to ride a bicycle. He was shy, lacking in confidence, and quite passive. Other kids picked on him and teased him, and he learned to avoid them. His parents were divorced, and he and his brother lived with their mom. His brother was a year younger, and he had been riding his bike for a couple of years!

As Dan's school counselor, it occurred to me one day that I could teach him to ride a bike, particularly if there were no other kids (especially his younger brother) around. I telephoned his mom and made arrangements with her and with the school to go with him to his house during the school lunch hour, and we would practice riding his bike. Within a few trials, he was riding, and the smile on his face told the whole story. His spirits were soaring! I didn't put a fancy label on it, like creating the self as model, but that's what it was. It was as helpful as any intervention I've ever had a hand in. At school and in the neighborhood Dan became more confident, and since he was getting to be a tall boy for his age, his size and new-found confidence carried him away from teasing and into friendships and belonging with a group of his peers.

As we get stronger, we find courage to try new things, and our belief about ourselves becomes *"I can do it if I try."*

> *... counselling brings healing because it offers affirmation of being, freedom from judgment and the strengthening that comes from being understood.*
>
> — Brian Thorne (1998)

Compassion Beyond Techniques

Compassion is the gift that nurtures the wounded spirit of our clients. The foundation of this compassion is believing in the essential goodness and potential within all human beings. Consciousness of our own *soul* allows us to recognize the *soul* within others and to know this to be the core of a person that is moving toward well-being.

When we as caregivers truly understand that compassion is the *soul* of our work, and when we integrate this into our personal ways of being, we will revolutionize the counseling professions. Our work will come from a place of love and a place of wisdom and clarity.

Integrating a spiritual perspective means going beyond a superficial level. Lisa, a former student wrote,

It is from this perspective that I want to approach all my relationships. Caring from a spiritual place is analogous to caring from a place of genuineness, integrity, love and authenticity, which I believe are essential counselor characteristics.

For too long, we have emphasized that counseling is about techniques, theories, or methodologies, and that these create optimal development if used effectively in our work. These at their very best are only the framework for the delivery of our gifts of the human spirit. Our focus on efficient techniques and such must not sacrifice our regard for the depth of our humanness. Carl Jung (1933) put it clearly:

There are ways which bring us nearer to living experience, yet we should beware of calling these ways "methods." The very word has a deadening effect. The way to experience, moreover, is anything but a clever trick; it is rather a venture which requires us to commit ourselves with our whole being. (p. 332).

Sometimes there are important but more subtle messages of our human spirit that are found in silence. Some examples of these are when we observe a client's eyes becoming moist as he fights back tears, or when we hear the deeper message behind the story and notice the voice breaking with emotion or softening to a whisper as he struggles to maintain composure. We need to acknowledge the depth of these moments because these are the expressions from their *soul*. Our clients will be more deeply touched by our thoughtful non-judgmental listening than by any intellectual explanation we might make. It may be simply a pat on the back as the client is leaving, which signals acknowledgment and encouragement, that turns the tide. It is our caring and respect that are felt deeply by a discouraged person.

To focus on the *soul* of a person is not easy in our culture. It may seem too personal, too invasive, and in that sense too threatening.

Because of our own social conditioning not to be invasive, we may inadvertently aid our clients in escaping from their *soulful* domain (e.g., by focusing too much on specific behavior and the surface details of their stories.) While it is not a good idea to be invasive, it is also a good idea not to be remote, unavailable, and aloof. We need to engage with our clients. If we don't engage, we are not fully present.

❖ *Soul Searching Journal Assignments — for Your Clients, and for Yourself*

- How might you sabotage yourself from getting what you want in life?
- Where do you stand with regard to the counselor's transparency, congruence and appropriate self-disclosure?
- Think of a time you trusted your intuition and what the results were.

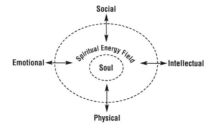

6

Wellness and Spiritual Integration

What is it that's getting well if not the soul?

We experience *wellness* as a balance of mind, body and spirit, a sense of wholeness. Our thoughts, our emotions and our behavior all seem to be working in complementary and supportive ways. Like a well-crafted quilt, we are all in one piece. With this integration, there is clarity, and often there is joy.

We all know people who exemplify wellness. They seem to radiate health and vitality. They laugh easily and love generously, with genuine compassion.

When insult, injury or illness come upon us, all our systems react to restore homeostasis. Healing from such negative events starts instantly, and occurs naturally and unconsciously, because we are genetically programmed for health in order to survive. But healing and preventing deterioration in health is greatly enhanced by a conscious effort and willingness to *choose* a healthy life style. Such awareness and choice are matters of the inner life and may not be imposed by edict or rule from forces outside our *selves*. As we respond to the various demands of life, there will be times when the total organism will not be perfectly balanced, as we focus our energy on one or another of our intellectual, social, emotional, or physical tasks. But at the point of recognizing that the stress of one domain is pulling the system out of balance, there is the opportunity to choose.

Optimal health will most certainly involve choosing wisely in matters of nutrition, exercise, relationships, environment, safety, attitudes, and beliefs. All of these issues are of concern to those of us who are professionals in health and human services, whose job it is to contribute to the well-being of others. This is especially true within the fields of counseling and psychotherapy, where it is essential to take a wholistic view of client choices and behaviors.

❖ Conversations With the Soul

Like our clients, in every waking hour of each day, we have choices to make. One choice, of course, is not to choose. But making choices means facing the dilemmas of our options and the short- and long-term consequences of each. An important question is: "How do I access the inner wisdom that wants me to make the best choices for my optimal well-being?"

Opening the door to the inner life requires two simple beginning steps: One, that we continually ask ourselves questions such as: "Is this good for me?" or, "What is my best choice here?" The second requirement is to be patient and to listen for the answer. This will most often involve some waiting, since dilemmas are always complex. The rule is: Keep asking and keep waiting. In a sense, we are wrestling with our *souls*. On one hand, the voice of pleasure and immediate satisfaction is inviting us to eat, drink and be merry — which is very tempting. On the other hand, the wisdom of the *soul* voice wants to be heard and will raise serious questions about the pleasure choice, mostly related to long-range gratification and the values and meaning of various consequences.

This *soul* mediation is a much deeper issue than a simple struggle of *id* and *superego*. Once this channel is open, the dialogue can be very rich with options, none of which represent black and white, either/or outcomes. And the *soul* voice must not be confused with the voices of churches or governments, or with other injunctions from our broad landscape of cultural voices. The key is to open ourselves to the inner wisdom of the *soul*, because it is the cohesive and driving force of our mind-body intelligence.

Throughout our lives, we will all come face-to-face with the existential question: *"What is the meaning of my life"*? Our *soul* is our ultimate in-charge voice for deciding what is good for us in the long run.

❖ Defining Soul Wellness

In chapter seven of William Miller's (1999) book *Values, Spirituality and Psychotherapy*, Richards, Rector and Tjeltvelt remind us of the growing evidence that the values people hold can promote physical and psychological coping, healing and well-being. They argue that because of that, "… clients' spiritual values should be viewed as a potential resource in psychotherapy rather than as something that should be ignored."

Witmer and Sweeney (1992) present a wholistic model for wellness and prevention over the lifespan, pointing to a body of research which suggests that we would do well to reassess our current thinking in human development and our priorities in the delivery of our health services. Their article is a marker event in the counseling and psychotherapy professions, referencing the acknowledgement of our human spirit and the importance of wholistic integration for wellness. They summarize a 1990 report from the United States Public Health Service (USPHS) that notes, "The federal government spends more than seventy-five percent of its healthcare dollars caring for people with chronic disease, strokes and cancer. At the same time, less than one half of one percent is spent to prevent these same diseases from occurring." This spending discrepancy is all the more alarming since, *in the middle of the twentieth century*, the World Health Organization (WHO, 1958) defined health to include physical, mental and social well-being.

This wholistic view considers health as the state of being fully alive, not just the absence of infirmity or disease. It is heartening to know that spiritual well-being is now also included in this definition. It is our spiritual domain that is the cohesive force of integration so essential for wellness.

Let's consider this wholistic model of wellness in detail.

Six Domains Essential for Soul *Wellness*
....

1. Spiritual Awareness
2. Intimacy: Family and Friends
3. Physical Fitness
4. Appreciation for Cultural Gifts: Music, Art, Literature and History
5. Recreation and Renewal
6. A Purposeful Life

---

1. Spiritual Awareness

This is the key domain, the evolving process we must enter if we are to open to a whole picture of ourselves, our possibilities, and our best pathways. We need to acknowledge that there is an inner *self*, a *soul*, which will guide us beyond the ego of our daily coping. Discovering the voice of our own *soul* will require taking time out from the mad scramble of our daily lives. We need to find a place where we can calm ourselves and be open to receiving answers to our questions. It is in this calm searching, when there is a willingness to question and to listen, that we will find our inner wisdom.

In another article on spiritual wellness, Chandler, Holden and Kolander (1992) write that, "Spirituality is a natural part of being human and can be conceptualized in an understandable and practical fashion." They point out that observable change that is not accompanied by spiritual development may be especially vulnerable to recidivism, and suggest that,

> *Attention to spiritual health plays a major role in helping individuals maintain positive change. The dieter must internalize the new self as healthy and at the appropriate weight. The ex-smoker must internalize the new self as a nonsmoker. The workaholic must internalize the new self as a balanced individual.* (p. 171).

A growing number of us in western cultures have taken up Yoga to pursue the spiritual life in a disciplined way. In Yoga, it is believed that the body is a temple, and that taking care of one's self with respect is a duty. A quote from *The Sivananda Companion to Yoga* (2000) expresses this idea well:

> *The underlying purpose of all the different aspects of the practice of Yoga is to reunite the individual self (jiva) with the absolute or pure consciousness (Brahman) — in fact, the word Yoga literally means joining.* (p.15)

Spiritual awareness is, arguably, a necessary pre-condition for all the other five domains, because spiritual awareness makes it possible to know ourselves more fully and to know just how important all the other five domains are to the quality of our lives.

2. Intimacy: Family and Friends

It is within the bosom of our families and the warmth of our friends that we learn courage and caring, humor and sensitivity, gratitude and reverence and the ability to love one another. In the absence of a loving *soul* connection with family and friends, we are very much less likely to develop these qualities. We need the warm embrace from our most intimate relationships. This is not just a sentimental notion. We know intuitively from our inner wisdom as well as from research evidence that we all have a strong need for belonging and for intimacy.

Witmer and Sweeney (1992) summarize several research findings on the important relationship between social support, interpersonal relationships and health. Among others:

- A ten-year study of 2,754 adults in Michigan revealed that those persons with the least social contacts had two to four times the mortality rate of the better socially connected.
- Loneliness, when it is an enduring condition of estrangement or social rejection, is associated with such variables as depression, suicide, alcohol abuse, anxiety, adolescent delinquency, poor self-concept, and increased mortality.
- Married women have better immune functioning than unmarried women, and women who reported they were happily married had the healthiest immune system of all the groups (p. 145).

We don't need to continue to research this question, any more than we need to re-invent the wheel. The message is clear:

there is a power in love, and it is spiritual power from the soul of one to the soul of another. The intimacy of laughter and crying, human touch, and the sense of belonging, acceptance and caring from those who love us, all heal us and nurture us. These are essential for life.

3. Physical Fitness

Our body is our temple,
it's all we truly have,
and as far as we know,
it's the only one we get!

— dw

Every day we are confronted with choices: to ride or walk, to salt our food or not, to add sugar or not, to take the elevator or walk the stairs, to glob on butter or not, and so on and on. Shall I have a second helping? Shall I have dessert? Shall I be a couch potato? And these are only the minor temptations or vices we face. Tobacco, alcohol, other addictive drugs — even pain medications — all call us to get high, to be cool, to alter our state of consciousness, to escape from immediate stress or pain, and to be accepted by our peers. So we think.

Disciplined: To be or not to be... If your client feels guilty for being a couch potato, it is because he is betraying himself by neglecting what his *soul* is asking of him for his body maintenance and health. Exercise should be like brushing teeth, a habit we do fairly easily (without great sacrifice) on a regular basis. Exercise is enhanced if it's fun, and push-ups and other things that are good for us can be fun also, if our attitude is open to making them so.

Walking is terrific because there is something natural and spiritual inherent in transporting ourselves this way. The rhythms of walking sent an unconscious message to the ancient roots of our brain when we took our first upright steps in an evolutionary leap, distinguishing our humanness.

Talk to your body and ask it what it needs. Your *soul* will answer in clear and specific truths if you listen attentively and with patience. The important question is, are you willing to make a plan in response to these truths? It may be exercise, nutrition or breaking old habits that are harmful. Our *soul* self wants us to be healthy because survival and self-fulfillment favor it. How do we find a balance and a rhythm that entails some discipline but not obsession, some schedule but not compulsion?

I like what fitness guru and author George Shehan said a few years ago in a talk at the University of New Hampshire, "First be a good animal." He emphasized that if we are dull and sluggish in our physical domain, we will not have optimal mental clarity. Our ability to respond effectively depends upon our overall sense of well-being, and this means we need to be physically strong and relatively free from spiritual turmoil.

In the helping professions, our own psychosocial issues should not get in the way of competence in our professional relationships and responsibilities. Spiritual health is the key to our integration and wholeness, and requires of us the discipline to maintain a high degree of awareness and a balanced perspective about our physical, mental, social, and emotional life. Such *soul wellness* is what we want for our clients. As counselors, we should not ask less for ourselves.

4. Appreciation for Cultural Gifts of Music, Art and Literature

I don't mean here that we all have to be scholars in the classics. It is that our well-being is enhanced when we allow ourselves to appreciate beauty, history and the philosophical and moral underpinnings of our culture. My spirit can be touched deeply by a painting or sculptured piece, by a wide range of music, and by theater, poetry, ballet, opera, and literature, among other experiences. One of the elements in this spiritual connection for me is that I am transported — or maybe it is more accurate to say *trance*-ported — into the immediacy of the moment by the artistry.

When I was in high school, someone pointed me to the *Rubaiyat* by Omar Khayyam, a twelfth century Persian poet and philosopher who spoke to me in metaphors about living life fully and being in the here and now of my existence.

> *Here with a Loaf of Bread beneath the Bough*
> *a flask of Wine, a Book of Verse — and Thou*
> *beside me, singing in the Wilderness*
> *and Wilderness is Paradise now!*

I learned from this beautiful metaphor about the sweetness of the juices of life, and to not let the opportunity of the moment pass me by.

Recently, I went to see and hear a performance of *The Sound of Music*, with my wife Leslie and our daughter Julia. This was recreation, art, music *and* literature, as well as wonderful family time... all food for my *soul*. I'm always amazed at how theater and music can move me. In our culture, men aren't supposed to cry, but the tears welled up in me and it felt wonderful to be so moved. When the Reverend Mother tells Marie to find her own way, and breaks into singing... *"Climb every mountain, ford every stream,"* she was singing to me, telling *me* to climb every mountain and ford every stream.

It's interesting that we tease each other about feeling so deeply, as if there is something wrong with it. I think it's our own embarrassment with letting ourselves be spiritually moved in public ("thank God it was dark in the theater!"). It's our way of hiding from ourselves and pretending to be strong; kind of silly when you think about it!

Another piece of *soul* touching for me in that performance was when Captain Von Trapp sang *Edelweiss*. Here is this stoic man standing up to Nazi Germany, refusing to be taken in like so many others, and singing this Austrian Folk song about an Alpine flower. His script calls for him to get "choked-up" (notice how we avoid the words spiritually moved), as he comes to the words, *"Bless our homeland forever."* I realized in an instant the bitter-sweetness of this highly evolved culture facing the threat of loss as it was about to be caught up in the evil maelstrom of Nazi Germany. This kind of story telling and theater that has evolved over thousands of years speaks directly to our *souls*.

Yet another personal example: I recently read Jean Auel's (1980) *Clan of the Cave Bear*, and my spirit was touched by the stories of these early cave people who roamed the earth in tribes and lived with elaborate social order. Auel brought the cave people vividly to life with her creative writing. When I read about the sacred ceremonies conducted by the clan to express their gratitude to the Gods for the success of the hunt, I see the roots of our own reverence and thanksgiving. When she tells about the gathering with distant clans for contests in foot racing and the throwing of spears in the hunt, I see the origins and heritage of our early and modern competitive games, such as the Olympics.

All these art forms enrich my life and give breadth to my appreciation for those who so eloquently share their wisdom. From the cave artists of our early primitive ancestors in France, to our current folk singers and songwriters, we are connected spiritually to each other by these creative expressions of our humanness.

5. Recreation and Renewal

... to be healthy is to have our energy circulating freely throughout all aspects of our being.

— John Welwood (2000)

There are several reasons that I love to golf, not the least of which is that it is played in a place of great natural beauty. I feel blessed, thankful for my health, and for my friendships with my golf buddies. For me, golf is fun. Conversation is lighthearted; sometimes this is just the ability to laugh at ourselves for a missed shot or a corny joke. Camaraderie is truly the gorp in life on such occasions — that special treat of sharing the serendipitous bonds of friendship. Of course, the challenge of trying to hit an accurate shot plays a role in drawing me into the game.

Another refreshing and renewing experience for me is swimming. It is a Saturday as I write, and in a few minutes, I am going to go for a swim in the lake with Leslie and Julia. Our neighbor Ginny may join us. She is ninety! What a great teacher she is for all of us about taking care of ourselves. She still works out at the gym, bicycles, walks, swims, kayaks, and reaches out to neighbors for social and recreational activities. There is no end to the variety of things that we may do to re-create — literally to renew our spirit.

Play is built into our genetic code for such renewal. Dogs are a good example of playfulness in animals. Our neighbor D. J. (a black lab) comes down often to see if I will throw a stick in the water for him to fetch. My arm gets tired long before his swimming tires him. Intense exercise, playing hard and having fun, purges the body of toxins and stimulates muscle cells as oxygen is pumped in to freshen every fiber of our being. It helps us get the cobwebs out of our brains as we consciously or unconsciously immerse ourselves in activities as we seek balance.

Genuine recreation demands a certain "letting go." If our participation has any pretense, such as the cultural valuing of being "cool," "pretty," "macho" or any other such stereotypical and sterile role, we will be pulled off center. Knowledge of what balance means in life, and the discipline to be a healthy chooser, deserve our continuous attention in the face of life's pressures and distractions. Taking recreation time, and "letting go" of our chores and responsibilities for that time, enormously enhances our perspective for self-understanding and well-being.

6. A Purposeful Life

We are all here to serve humanity in one way or another. Our true purpose is to contribute to the well-being and well-functioning of the whole of our community. We become misguided and fail to clearly see our purpose when we get caught up in greed and material gain. Genuine satisfaction in life comes when we know that there is meaning in what we do, even if it is but a small contribution to making our community a better place to live. Some people are called to serve in high-risk circumstances, some in creative ways, some in high-profile activities, and others in everyday tasks nonetheless heroic. All are contributing.

As counselors, social workers, nurses, doctors, therapists and others in the helping professions, we find our meaning and pleasure in helping people. Somehow, caregiving helps us make sense of our lives. Our need to serve may come from the wounds of our earlier years, or from having learned by witnessing others who treat each other badly. Our evolutionary instinct to survive tells us that there must be a better way. If we are fortunate, we will find a hero, a model or a mentor to emulate and help us find our path.

My own search for a purposeful life probably started with my being upset about my father's alcoholism and the poor communication between my father and mother. I knew somehow that things did not need to be this way. As I grew into adulthood, I also knew that I did not want to repeat or continue in this pattern.

Despite his having a serious problem with alcohol for a number of years, there was much that was positive about my Dad, and he was a good model for me in many ways. He was a great appreciator of the outdoors from his own direct experience of our western frontier. Growing up on a small dirt farm in Oklahoma, he learned to hunt and to fish and to preserve meat by drying it, curing it in a smokehouse, or with salt. He grew up seeing that the whole family contributed, and neighbors helped each other gather crops and prepare them for storage in the cellar because there was no refrigeration. My dad always said when we went camping: *"We will leave this campground cleaner and better than we found it."* This injunction became a metaphor for life for me: *"I will leave this planet a better place than it was when I got here."* Of course, this is a little grandiose, but my efforts have nonetheless been duty-bound to some extent by that code. I realized in my later years that my father had many good qualities. My experience reminds me a little of what Mark Twain allegedly said about his father: "When I was a boy of seventeen, I thought my father was so ignorant I could hardly stand to have the old man around. But when I got to be twenty-one, I was astonished at how much the old man had learned in just four years."

Roadblocks to Wellness: Negative Spiritual Energy

There are obstacles in our pathway to wellness that will set us back and put us out of balance. When we encounter toxic energy directed at us from another person, we are forced to cope with it in one way or another. Here are some examples of such toxic energy that can wound our *soul*.

- criticism, negative evaluation or judgment
- discouragement
- being treated with apathy or indifference
- being surrounded by people who are cynical and pessimistic
- being under-acknowledged or devalued
- betrayal
- rejection

These all represent various aspects and degrees of psychological abuse, and all are capable of causing damage to the psyche *(soul)* of the person receiving such negativity. Any such negativity will have a poisonous effect on the spirit, and will require the rallying of the strength of our *soul* resources if we are to find wellness. Certainly the antidotes will be found in relationships which are loving and where we feel accepted, understood, validated and respected.

Depending on the level of severity and significance of toxic persons in an individual's life, counseling or psychotherapy may well be a necessary support to restore balance and perspective.

Individuals who fail to successfully work through the spiritual damage inflicted in these ways may:

- close themselves off from others
- become bitter and spiteful
- seek revenge and retaliation
- be prejudiced and intolerant of others
- be selfish and greedy
- be jealous and envious
- become hateful people themselves
- be disposed to cause harm in some way to themselves or to others.

We need to be passionately disciplined in helping our clients to challenge these toxic roadblocks if they are to overcome their negative impact and open doors for making healthy choices.

❖ *Melody — The Gift of Our Work Being Acknowledged*

As counselors, on our purposeful paths we don't always know when we may help our clients reverse some of the toxic patterns in their lives. And if somehow we discover that we may have contributed in a small way to touching someone's life, it is an enormous gift.

One of the most validating acknowledgments in my long career was a letter from a former eighth-grade student named Melody. I had been her counselor throughout junior high school, and kept trying to help her as she continually got herself in trouble with her teachers and parents. She was a bright girl, and I had faith in her that she would turn around her negative behavior. Ten years later she found my address at the university and in her letter she said, *"I am just wanting to reach out and thank all those who helped me along the way, and you were one of those. I am an attorney now, and realize I might not have gotten this far without your help. Thank you!"*

It has been twenty-five years since I received that letter. I was myself touched in return, and it renewed my faith that my efforts can make a difference. Emily Dickinson put it well:

> *If I can stop one Heart from breaking,*
> *I shall not live in vain;*
> *If I can ease one Life the Aching,*
> *Or cool one Pain,*
> *Or help one fainting Robin*
> *Unto his Nest again,*
> *I shall not live in Vain.*
> — Emily Dickinson (1951)

❖ *Soul Searching Journal Assignments — for Your Clients, and for Yourself*

- Ask your *soul:* "What do I need to do for my next steps of growth?" Listen for your *soul* to speak, and write your answers.
- Rate yourself with a score of 1 through 5 on the Six Domains Essential for *Soul* Wellness (with 5 being the highest). Reflect awhile on each and then write a paragraph about (a) What has been good for you to nourish your *soul*, (b) What you will choose to do for growth. Write down a date you will start, and commit to it.
- Think of a person, an event, or a time when you experienced each of the negative roadblocks to wellness. (a) Jot down a name or time for each off the top of your head, then go back and write a short recall, (b) What you would say to that person now, and, (c) Write yourself instructions on what you need to do to let it go and let yourself forgive.

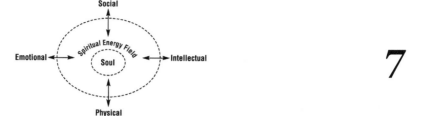

7

No Numbers and Categories
What Role for Assessment?

For some, assessing (let alone measuring)
spirituality sounds like an oxymoron.
— Ronald Gorsuch and
William Miller (1999)

The *soul* cannot be captured by boundary markers. No net may be cast to contain it. In therapeutic counseling there is no linear or quantitative measurement of the *soul*. We need to acknowledge that we don't have to measure everything. An act of kindness, for example, is a spiritual gift, and is to be experienced with savoring and rejoicing. Why try to reduce it to numbers? Such natural acts of love are too full of wonder to quantify.

We can only really know what our clients are willing to tell us, but we can make further assumptions from our impressions of voice tone, posture, vitality (or lack of it), affect, facial expressions (particularly the mouth, and eyes). We glean much information from ongoing and comprehensive observation of the person. It is a qualitative and global assessment, and is ultimately about the quality or wellness of the *soul* of the person.

Constance Fischer (2001), whose focus on assessment was away from objectification and toward life in the real world, speaks of her early work as being grounded in European existential and phenomenological philosophy. She writes:

When engaging in psychological assessment, I anticipate being able to describe patterns relevant to the purposes of assessment, but I do not undertake to explain in terms of traits, categories or causes... All evidence is directly available to the senses, not probabilistic or deductive (p. 31)

The "life world orientation" of which Constance Fischer writes is the lens for assessment in matters of the *soul*, because it considers whole persons and the context of their lives. She puts it this way:

... Our findings are not scores or categories, but rather are revised understanding in relation to specific questions, of how the person has been going through life; findings include personally viable alternative pathways that the person might take. The assessments life world orientation allows the client to participate actively throughout the assessment. (p. 31)

In our attempts to be a legitimate behavioral science, our profession has yielded to our statistically minded colleagues, whose demand for evidence and accountability discounted intuitive nuances of meaning in experience. Fischer reminds us that,

Early psychologists adopted the methods of emerging natural sciences, despite pleas from philosophers such as Dulthey (1894-1977) that psychology should align itself with the sciences of spirit and mind, and of warnings from philosophers such as Hussard (1935-1937-1970) about the dangers of psychology becoming a technology. (p. 30)

In spite of these warnings, psychology in the western world has followed the research model of the natural sciences. As a result, we have taken microscopic rather than macroscopic views of human behavior.

In a major address to the American Psychological Association, Ron Fox (2003), a former president of APA, admonished the profession for its fascination with the small fluff of irrelevant details. As psychologists, he suggested, we should be more concerned with how to prevent war, deal with poverty, cope with racism and reduce human misery than with the truly petty questions. He had the courage to advise us to deal with the big issues, including *"the healing power of human love."*

We have designed paradigms and assessment tools attempting to explain intellect, emotion, social and physical phenomena. We have organized diagnostic categories in an attempt to classify abnormal behavior, often without sufficient anchor points as to what is "normal." We need to remember that most norm-referenced testing favors "white culture." Achievement and aptitude measures are based on a bell-shaped curve, most often with little or no consideration to the cultural diversity of the general population. In our multicultural world, we can't afford such hegemony if we are to stand for justice and equality.

Quantification and categorization are simply irrelevant to the important cultural experiences that shape our *souls*. When one considers, within each culture, the spiritual experiences of birth, friendship, family, intimacy, marriage, and personal loss, it is clear that these most-human events are beyond a linear or sequential summary of the details of our lives. Our spiritual human experiences need not be measured. Miller and Thoreson (1999) write: "Like personality and health, spirituality is complex. It is not adequately defined in any single continuum or by dichotomous classifications; rather, it has many dimensions.... This avoids the misleading classification of people as 'spiritual' versus 'not spiritual', or as more versus less spiritual." In this regard, Richards, Rector and Tjeltveit (1999) remind us that it is not a matter of nailing down and an exact definition of a person on some spiritual scale but rather more to the point that we gain an understanding of our client's world view and core values.

Over time, we see the deeper *soul* struggles in the lifestyle choices which our clients make. For example:

- Fitness or illness
- Alcohol use in balance or out-of-control
- Congeniality or isolation from others

Self-reporting, as in the "Client Self-Reporting Forms" (see the Appendix) is a useful tool because it is a direct invitation for clients to focus and clarify their own inner life of values and meaning. Gordon Allport once said, if you want to know something about a person, ask.

While spirituality is not assessed in formal or traditional terms, we nonetheless need to acknowledge assessment as a taking in of our total sensing of the person as we observe and try to understand. Gorsuch and Miller (1999) point out, "One simple reason for attending to spirituality is that variables in this domain have been widely known to be predictive of health outcomes." They go on to say:

> ... *clinicians ought to be interested in at least a basic understanding of clients' spirituality much as one assesses other risk and protective factors such as family history, social support, and stress.... A second reason for understanding clients' spirituality is that regardless of it's relationship to presenting problems, for many people it is an important or even central element of their larger world views and life context within which presenting concerns will be addressed.... Clients may bring a broad range of spiritual beliefs and coping resources, ranging from private personal practices (such as prayer or meditation) to involvement in supportive religious communities.* (pp. 48-49).

Richards, Rector and Tjeltveit (1999) emphasize that there is growing evidence that people's spiritual values and behavior can promote healing and well-being. Isn't it clear that these spiritual values are the very core of the person? To ignore these in any assessment of our clients is to pay attention only to the outer symptoms while disregarding the underlying causes, and essential foundations that shape our life choices. We are essentially spiritual beings, and assessment in traditional formal formats is not sufficient. Standardized instruments and procedures focus on specific aspects of the person, not the whole of the person. I'm not suggesting that we should throw out all assessment that attends to the details of interests, attitudes, or personality characteristics; much of this can be useful. But we need as well a more global assessment that will help us see the bigger picture of our clients. We need greater understanding of their unique history, context, and current concerns as we work with them in the counseling relationship.

Assessment Should Be Informal, Continuous, and Transparent

Informal. Formal assessment often engenders defensiveness and fear of judgment, raises anxiety and tension, disrupts rapport, and erodes trust, as clients understand that they are being evaluated and compared to others. Under these conditions, how could we get a clear picture of a whole person in a therapeutic setting? Any assessment by the therapist should be user-friendly with full disclosure to the client of what you are wondering about as you gather this information, and why. Therapists should be clear of their own motives to be sure that any information gathering will yield value for the client. If any formal assessment needs to be done, it should not be done by the person who will be acting as the therapist, lest it start the relationship with hierarchy and fear of judgment.

I usually open my counseling sessions with a general open-ended question such as, "What's happening that's of concern in your life?" It is an invitation to focus our work on what is important to my client. There is no direction, no reference to the work of previous sessions, and none of my agenda or priorities for the use of our time together. If my client fails to respond to this invitation, I might add, *"I am imagining that you have some ideas of what you want to explore and work on today."* This neutrality is a little like a walk in the fog, inviting the client to be my guide.

Sometimes we have to wait patiently in dealing with the clients' resistance, holding ourselves back from filling the silent space with questions from our agenda. While such questions might be relevant, the danger is that we nurture their resistance by giving them our structure. Our informal assessment of our clients comes from our sensitive observations of their behavior, their resistance, their tone of voice and body posture, and the underlying spirit as they share their stories.

Continuous. Our work in counseling requires us continually to observe and take readings from our clients. "What is that tear about"? "I noticed your voice change as you spoke of your loss."

"I get a sense from your facial expression and posture that you're a little down right now." These kinds of out-loud musings with clients give us an opportunity to be both congruent and transparent. It's an invitation for them to clarify, expand and discover. Continuous assessment provides current data regarding the clients' overall emotional tone, their social and relationship experiences, and the larger existential life concerns that may be surfacing for them. It also allows us to remain tentative and open as we check out our hunches with a client. These observations are fluid, and not simply a fixed or categorical process.

Transparent. I want to be open and fully present with my clients in order to hear and to sense their deeper inner feelings arising from the wounds of their *souls*. I want to be transparent, holding no hidden agendas. I want to respond with compassion, and I want to challenge and invite my clients to explore the origins of their pain. If I fail to challenge and invite in-depth exploration, I may be colluding with the client's cover-up. If I am overly concerned about protecting my clients, I may be entering into co-dependence and complicity with their resistance to go to the source of their pain. If I am just putting on a band-aid, I will need to examine my own resistance to entering into the depth of my client's *soul*.

Whatever my intervention choice, I want to have my motives understood by my client, I want to be, as Rogers put it, "transparently real."

❖ Accountability and Assessment

Increasingly I have found myself becoming imprisoned in a vicious circle of feverish activity as the new accountability culture permeates the world of therapy.
— Brian Thorne (1998)

While we must work within the policies of the agency or institute, bureaucracy must not dictate our priorities nor cause us to sacrifice our basic humanity. Our primary accountability must be to our clients, our constituents, and ourselves, in the context of our professional standards. These are issues of ethical significance, to which I hold myself accountable as I assess my own performance as well as the movement of my client. Just as a gardener moves freely in tilling the soil, pulling weeds, cultivating and irrigating, so must I till the *soul*, observing, responding, challenging, and encouraging my clients to create optimal growing conditions for themselves. But if my work is only geared to being accountable to the assessment of my supervisor, or to compliance with the demands of a health insurance organization, my focus and achievement efforts will be on external rewards or bureaucratic policies, my more intuitive sense of the whole person will be compromised. While I understand the requirements for policies that are designed to protect both client and counselor, I believe the bureaucracies tend to squeeze the personal characteristics out of the formula and diminish the humanness of the exchange. I'm sure that standardizing these procedures helps to reduce paperwork and ease decision making, but we must not let such reductions impinge on our own respect for the person we call *client*, nor compromise the integrity of our own character.

If not the bureaucracy's ideas of assessment, then, what if any procedures do I advocate? Here are some of the tools that work for me...

- Observation
- Active Listening and Reflection Inquiry
- Process Notes
- Client Self-Assessment and Written History
... and a couple that do not
- Cumulative Records in School
- Faculty Lounge Assessment

Observation

> *Life events are the primary data.*
> — Constance Fisher

As therapists, we must be keen observers of our own *soul* voices and our own life issues, in order to be clear, present and comfortable with the depths of our clients' explorations. Observing the client as we counsel, we need to develop and hold a "beginner's mind." There is no normative template that we overlay on our clients to see if there is a misfit, nor do we attempt to squeeze them into any spurious pre-existing molds. Without the blank slate of a beginner's mind, we will not serve our clients' growth potential because we draw boundaries around them. Better to enter our work with hope and confidence (faith) in their inner wisdom and inclination to grow.

Our observations must have a panoramic contextual perspective in considering all the light, color, texture, history and culture of our clients' unique experience. Because of this complexity and uniqueness, assessment in matters of the *soul* needs to take a tentative avenue of inquiry and reflection, always communicating great respect for the person. Our goal is to remain open, and not to seek to arrive at absolute or fixed conclusions.

❖ Active Listening and Reflection Inquiry

In our culture, we have learned to mask our true feelings because we learn that there is risk in being vulnerable. But when the masks go on, our authentic and congruent *self* remains hidden. It is the job of therapeutic counseling to create safety for the *soul* of the client to emerge into light. It was Tom Gordon (1970) who coined the term "active listening" in his book, *Parent Effectiveness Training (P.E.T.)*. He studied with Carl Rogers and built on Rogers' ideas of reflecting deeper feelings. Gordon instructed us to get beneath the surface expression to discover the deeper meanings of our clients.

Here's an example of an active listening response:

What I just heard you say Mitch, was that on one hand you are okay with being laid off from work, but on the other 'unspoken' hand, I sense that there is some considerable hurt that is not so easy to talk about. I sense this from the sadness of your tone of voice, your facial expression and your body posture. I suspect that you are more hurt by the job loss than you care to admit, and feeling a bit down. Am I getting that right?

Readers can see that listening to body language is every bit as important as hearing the verbal message.

It is this tentative but active inquiry that allows me to check with my clients to see if I am accurate in my reflections. In so doing, I invite them to validate or clarify their deeper feelings. Presenting feedback and challenging clients to go more deeply into their *soul* issues is often awkward because we are all socially enculturated to keep things safe, to not go into vulnerable places. While active listening seems straightforward and quite simple, it requires discipline and training to listen deeply and respond appropriately to these inner feelings. It is the meaning behind the content that we want to get to.

Sometimes our responses to our clients should be purposely vague. If we are not clear, and admit it, our vagueness and uncertainty invites the client to clarify and to specify, thus helping us to understand. For example: *"I'm not quite sure what it is you're saying here, can you help me out?"* This uncertainty takes us off the expert pedestal and empowers our clients to claim their own discoveries of *self*. As they clarify for us, they become more clear themselves.

In a sense, *soul* counseling is not new; there have always been those whose genuine empathy made contact with the core issues of the self, and as I mentioned in earlier chapters, Carl Rogers was probably the first *soul* counselor. But the *soul* connecting work that we do is larger than a single element such as empathy. It is never a technique, and always an attitude and an emphasis that is overarching and integrative. It is a deeper level of inquiry that will open to a more global sense of the person and his core *soul* issues. It is a way of looking at things differently, through a spiritual lens.

❖ *Process Notes*

As part of being accountable for my work, I think it is a good idea to write down summary impressions after each session. This may be just a few sentences, questions or a short paragraph, but it allows me to track the issues of my concern, and serves as a reference for reviewing our work together. Whatever is written is available to the client upon request. Nothing hidden! If a diagnosis must be made to conform to agency or managed care or insurance requirements, this diagnosis is made with the client's knowledge, understanding and acceptance.

❖ Cumulative Records in Schools

While the information within school files can be helpful, it can also encourage a label attachment to a student, and labels are difficult to shed. Recorded information, like a photograph, falls short of capturing the whole story. Anecdotal records are impressions, and while they may be helpful, they may also be a history that is developmentally outgrown. I instruct my graduate students not to look at cumulative records until after they have met their clients. I want them to begin with an open mind, with no preconceived ideas or judgments. Gaining knowledge of students prior to meeting them may contaminate impressions and overall assessment. There is always the danger of pegging the student into some categorical slot that can only restrict her freedom to move beyond the expectations of others.

For this same reason, I believe that teachers should not see the files until they have met the student, unless it is deemed necessary in planning for remedial or pro-active interventions. Many teachers may have taught an older sibling, and they become vulnerable to a mind-set that poisons the neutrality of their impressions about the incoming younger sibling. Readers would be well served to read the classic book, *Pygmalion in the Classroom* (1968), to understand the power of expectations and self-fulfilling prophecies.

❖ Faculty Lounge Assessment

Nothing is worse than the gossip, labeling and categorizing that often goes on in faculty lounges as teachers and staff members share their frustrations and prejudices about students. Judgmental and stereotyping comments contaminate all within earshot. These toxic exchanges, can't help but leach out in a prejudiced way against the student and have negative effects.

❖ The Audacity of Labeling

Most insurance and managed care companies will require a diagnosis from the current *DSM* from those of us working in community mental health or private practice. Such determinations must be made with great care, of course, and should be done openly, with the full participation and understanding of our clients. These long-distance bureaucratic treatment decisions about therapy hold little regard for the person-to-person *soul* connection so essential for healing and growth.

Labeling people with diagnostic categories can be particularly reductionistic and insulting. There is a certain arrogance in placing complex human beings into simple categories. Such pigeonholing can be extremely hurtful to a person with low self-esteem. Many of our clients come to us with considerable self-doubt and negative self-talk. To stick a label on a wounded *soul* can in no way be helpful.

Here's what a client of mine wrote about being labeled:

To say to someone — you are schizophrenic, you are borderline... can be harmful. Labels impose restrictions, unnecessary restrictions, on a person. I can almost understand how labeling a person helps a doctor or institution to be more in control — we know who/what you are and what to do to help you. But it seems like just another way to control someone who's already feeling powerless. Can't we just be people — maybe confused and scared at times — maybe with different realities — Oh shit, I can't say what I want to say. Labeling seems to have something to do with power and hierarchical structures and lack of trust and faith and respect. When a doctor labels a patient they can concentrate on how to treat the label instead of listening to the person. The categorization of the patient becomes the goal — the appropriate label must be sought and found in order to know what to do. What about listening? What about asking the patient what they need and want? What about seeing the client as an equal person who is experiencing pain? What about asking the client what will comfort them instead of presuming to know what they need? Labels hurt.

Labels will not help guide our clients on their path of self-discovery if the *essence* of their being is reduced to a category. We need to hold a vision of their potentials, not their limitations. We need to encourage them, and to help them build hope. As therapists, our responsibility is to help them find their strength within, and to discover that sense of self that wants to transcend, not just survive. What our clients really want is what everyone wants: *to be recognized as whole persons, to be acknowledged, cared about, and accepted in their process of becoming who they are*. If assessment is perceived as judgment or evaluation, it will threaten their *souls* and dampen their spirits.

Still I know, that in the real world, we are not yet at a place where we will just abandon our standard competent and ethical practice in assessment. We need to reconcile our need for *soul* understanding and connection with the requirements for DSM IV diagnosis and treatment plans that meet the current standard of managed care, along with the dictates of insurance companies regarding the number of sessions we have available for a particular client.

There are a number of ways we can work within the system.

1. Follow standard-of-care procedures, but emphasize *soul* in your work with clients.

2. Learn to apply DSM IV language to your *soul* counseling approach.

3. Explain the dilemma to your clients, and describe to them how you will work together, given the requirements of the system.

4. Advocate for change in your institution; convince your institution that your clients should be seen as people with *souls*, with less emphasis on numbers and diagnoses.

5. When formal diagnosis and treatment plans are required, add your more personal assessment comments as a supplement. I think this human touch would be very welcome by most readers of your reports.

6. Of course, if you are able to see only private-pay clients, you can keep your attention on their *soul* needs.

7. If your setting is simply too bureaucratic to be comfortable, or if you feel you are compromising your own *soul* in meeting

their requirements, look for work elsewhere, in a setting that is more hospitable to your needs.

This is not an either/or arena, it's a matter of emphasis and reconciling some of the distance and differences between two points of view. Certainly we must meet the reasonable demands of the "real" world, while at the same time trying to soften it with attention to the *psyche* in psychology.

The priorities of the issues are:

1. Following the ethical standards of care.
2. Meeting the individual needs of clients
3. Meeting the institutional requirements without compromising 1 and 2.

I have three very good friends who live and work in the very real world. Dr. Bert Whetsone is a child and family psychologist in private practice who also works and consults with schools on assessment and individual treatment plans. Dr. Jason Holder does adventure-based counseling with individuals, groups, and sometimes families, and Dr. Paul Treacy is a school psychologist who does mostly assessments of special needs children at all levels in school. None of them would call themselves *soul* counselors. but each of them have those human qualities and sensitivities that:

a) see the big picture of their clients in cultural and family context,

b) have great compassion and empathy for people generally and clients specifically, and most importantly,

c) have a gentle human touch with warmth and humor in all matters of their work. They are themselves good *souls* with balanced lives, all working within the professional system in creative ways.

It's not that you are either a "*soul* counselor" or not. I'm not looking to start another new title which separates people from each other. Rather, I'm hoping to integrate the ideas, the consciousness, the attitudes, and the willingness to see *soul* issues as central to our work — to see the *soul* in each person as the deeper sense of self.

I believe the greeting, *Namaste* from Hindu cultures comes closest to recognizing this spiritual quality. I am told that Namaste means, "I salute the divinity within you." It's a common greeting in certain eastern cultures, and a reminder to recognize our spiritual nature. Recently I opened my fortune cookie after a fine meal at a Chinese restaurant to find this message: "We are not human beings who are spiritual, we are spiritual beings who are human." I like that sentiment — and the cookie was good too! We *are* spiritual beings! Recognizing this will change the way you work and live.

In preparing this chapter, I found myself persuading my editor (himself a counseling psychologist) of my desire to be outspoken, outrageous, even revolutionary about this topic. I hope it will resonate well with you, and help you to wake up and take the courage to re-order your priorities. I don't want to water down my idealism too much and give you an easy rationalization for staying with the status quo. People will do what they need to do to survive in their jobs, but in time, the profession will come to see that some of the ways we deal with assessment (for example, dependence upon bell-shaped curves and norm references) are not built on multicultural populations, and are in fact very "white favorable." Moreover, there is nothing about most psychological assessment that has anything to do with a person's *soul*.

Dr. Sam Gladding, psychologist and professor at Wake Forest University, and 2004-2005 President of the American Counseling Association summed it up nicely (Gladding, 2004):

> *While diagnoses and labels may seem necessary at times, we need to remember that people are more complex than the words we use to describe them.*

Soul Searching Journal Assignments — for Your Clients, and for Yourself

- Make a list of at least twenty things that you do, or relationships you have, that give your life meaning. Write these quickly off to the top of your head, no monitoring. Now go back over your list and check the ones in which you are engaged on a regular basis. Reflect and write your thoughts and feelings on these choices.

- Think of any labels or names that have been attached to you by someone at sometime and write about how they made you feel.
- Think back to a time in school when you experienced being categorized or given a score on some test. Write about how this impacted your sense of self.

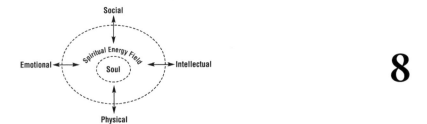

Social

Emotional ◄——► Intellectual

Physical

Spiritual Energy Field

Soul

8

When Soul Collides with Culture

In writing of how culture impacts the *soul* of counseling, I will look at culture in a broad perspective in this chapter, taking three divergent vantage points, as they impact the counseling process. Part One briefly reviews our multicultural awakening from the American fabric of racial, political, social, economic and educational disenfranchisement. Part Two takes a different and more detailed view, examining the many factors of culture and religion that shape who we are. Part Three places culture in the context of the counseling relationship, and offers a variety of examples of how our awareness, sensitivity, understanding and efforts to right the wrongs of discrimination has created some blind spots. It is important to acknowledge some of the pitfalls in our vigilance to be politically correct in multicultural considerations.

ONE: AWAKENING TO DISCRIMINATION AND HYPOCRISY

Thomas Jefferson wrote that "all men are created equal." While he spoke a great truth, he was in fact living a lie because he personally owned slaves. It was a bad example. It was another eighty-seven years before enough courage was gathered to address this great national travesty at the highest levels of government. But not even Abraham Lincoln's *Emancipation Proclamation*, and victory of the Union Army in the Civil War could erase the bigotry and shameful discrimination being perpetuated by large numbers of the Euro American white majority culture in the United States. Our history of prejudice and segregation has been an insult to the *soul* and the character of our American way of life, spilling toxic inequality into the lives of virtually all persons of color. In a separate but equally despicable way, this Euro American, white, male-dominated culture also relegated women to a lesser status in the larger scheme of the economic, political and social order. It wasn't until the African American racial revolution with the non-violent demonstrations in the 1960s, led by Dr. Martin Luther King Jr. and others, that there was consequential civil rights legislation and enforcement.

Wing-Sue, Ivey and Pederson (1996) summarized this well, with challenging questions:

> *The demand by racial/ethnic minorities and women for equal access and opportunities; the increasing awareness of the pervasiveness of racism, sexism, and oppression; and the Third World, Women's and Civil Rights movements coalesced to confront society with an unpleasant question: Are we an integrated nation that believes and practices equality for all, or are we a nation segregated and unequal? The honest answer to this question has raised numerous others as well. If we truly believe in the democratic principles we claim to hold so dearly, what must we do as a nation to achieve these goals?* (p. xvii)

Our "white culture" continues to have many hidden and not-so-hidden biases and discriminatory practices throughout our society. Again, Wing-Sue, Ivey and Pederson (1996) highlight some of the more blatant and painful shortcomings in the mental health professions.

> *Educational materials and research have portrayed minorities in negative stereotypes; an implicit equation has been made between pathology and different lifestyles of culturally different groups; mental health services have often culturally oppressed minority clients; and counselors and psychotherapists have failed to recognize the biased assumptions present in theories about human behavior.* (p. xvii)

Just as all cultures are time-bound and encapsulated by the boundaries of their mainstream norms, our forefathers and foremothers remained trapped by their cultures' negligence and apathy about moving toward the truly democratic values of freedom and equality. Our waking up is long overdue.

❖ *Free at Last*

Since Martin Luther King Jr. helped to wake us all up some forty-or-so years ago, we have worked hard in the helping professions and made significant gains in correcting our attitudes, and the shortcomings and omissions of our rather rigid theoretical foundations. We have infused cultural awareness and context into our curricula and training programs, but we're not there yet. Corey (2005) reminds us: "... to the extent that traditional theories disregard culture, they are outmoded and restrictive." He goes on to say that rather than having a separate multicultural theory, he favors "developing a multicultural perspective, which is an approach one can incorporate into the fabric of most contemporary theories" (p. 100). Corey suggests that theories can adapt by expanding their focus to include both individual and social factors, and that if culture is not a vital concern, our practice will remain encapsulated. He believes that, "The role of the counselor often includes teaching the client about underlying cultural dimensions to present concerns." (p. 108)

Before we can teach or counsel others, it is clear that counselors in training and continuing professional development must strive for self-awareness to understand the impact of their own cultural heritage, and recognize all the blind spots, stereotypes and other pre-conceived notions and prejudices that get in the way of an open, fair and non-judgmental mind.

TWO: THE SHAPING FORCES OF CULTURE

Each of us is born with a variety of genetic predispositions, but we are also very vulnerable to the culture that will define us and try to confine us. Our *soul* is present at birth but not yet formed. The norms, beliefs and traditions of our culture will be imposed upon us. Every facet of our culture and subcultures will shape us.

In addition to the values and mores of the larger culture, the very essence of who we are, our spirit, and all manifestations of our total being will be greatly affected by

- Family of origin and extended family
- Race and Ethnicity
- Socioeconomic status
- Gender
- Religion
- Educational level
- Career and occupational history
- Sexual orientation
- Political philosophy
- Community and nation of residence
- Emerging consciousness of globalization
- The age in which one lives.

All these subsets of culture reward those who are loyal, devout, and diligent. And the rewards increase if you are smart, attractive, athletic, cooperative, compliant, articulate, rich, trustworthy and responsible.

Most of these cultural subsets are predetermined by circumstances beyond our individual control. But as individuals continue their education and development, there will be those who will find themselves more able to choose, albeit still very much influenced by the norms of their particular cultural heritage. Our early choices are skewed toward conformity because we need to belong, to be safe, to be nurtured, and to gain a sense of identity. Finding our identity within the group is a major quest for meaning in our lives.

There can be no doubt that cultural forces powerfully impact what we believe and how we behave. Cultures define the rules and expect loyalty and adherence for membership.

To abandon membership in any of our subcultures is to run the risk of facing the powerful forces of rejection, ridicule, negative judgment, discrimination, ostracism, and in some cases physical abuse and even death. As counselors, it behooves us to try to understand and be sensitive to the multifaceted influences of culture.

❖ *The Gifts and Misgiving of Culture*

Culture is the lens and the filter for our beliefs, attitudes, values, and much of our behavior. Culture is our clothing, our house, our playing field of life and, in some cases, our prison. Our *souls* can either be nourished by our families, our communities and our institutions, or they can be squelched. Our *souls* are nourished when we are loved and accepted for our individuality and autonomy. Squelching and wet blankets arrive when we are made to conform to the authoritarian edicts of individuals, institutions or governments that would control our freedom with rigid rules.

Rigidity creates dualistic thinking: good or bad; right or wrong; black or white; "us" against "them." Such dualism may be seen in highly nationalistic and religious cultures that require total devotion, subservience, and party-line loyalty from their members. While the presumption is that this devotion is for the greater good, such rigid dictates are based on fear and a desire to control members of the culture — under the guise of protecting them and maintaining traditions. These xenophobic cultural injunctions portray outside influences as evil or dangerous, or both. Cultural traditions, based on fear and power, contaminate the *soul* because people within any culture, when they feel safe, will want to grow, and will want to be free in their choices.

Within our cultural milieu, we form links with kindred spirits. In the best of circumstances, our cultures offer the support of love, belonging, and a healthy sense of self within the group. If we are fortunate, we truly become *soul* brothers, *soul* sisters, and *soul* mates. It is in this context of families and neighbors that we discover love and our deepest sense of connection to life. Compassion, caring, respect and encouragement all nourish the *soul* and help us to forge a healthy sense of who we are in the larger world.

Cultures are like rivers, changing only slowly as erosion wears away stubborn obstacles. While cultures are made stable by long-held values and traditions, they also must flex and evolve with time and events. In cultures that discourage or disallow individual freedom, where self-expression is not safe, the individual *soul* will be stifled. Blind loyalties that cause us to forsake our own sense of morality, will contaminate our *souls*. Severe restrictions of freedom that have been handed down by the voices of earlier generations must be cast away like worn-out shoes. Over time, these rigidities of intolerance will no longer be appropriate or functional because they impede our evolution. We need to learn to say "No thank you, these rules don't apply in our world today."

For the *soul* to develop, there must be freedom. We all know from personal experience that:

- Our spirit *soars* with freedom and encouragement
- Our spirit *sours* with prohibitive restrictions and discouragement

When I look back and reflect on the events of the twentieth century, and our evolution from horses and buggies to space travel and communication satellites, I am in awe of the changes that continue to impact *all* people of our earth. All humans living on our planet are swept along to greater or lesser degrees with the enormous forces of change wrought by technology and consequent commerce. One doesn't need to reference the demographic data in the United States to know that there are massive cultural shifts within our country. People of color or mixtures of color are already in the majority in many regions. As we evolve, we need to retain and embrace those cultural characteristics that honor our many heritages: music, dance, visual art, crafts, costume, cuisine, and the history of our ceremonies and rituals. But all cultures need to transcend those facets of their history and tradition that engender prejudice and intolerance toward those who are different. As we discard ignorance and embrace tolerance, we will let go of our blind loyalty to those ideals that foster hatred toward a particular race, religion, or gender. The challenge for each of us in all our various sub-cultures is to find the path of harmonious evolution.

When we are not impeded by a restrictive authoritarian culture, our *souls* will come down on the side of freedom, peace and compassion. There is a natural tendency for healthy human beings to be compassionate toward one another, and when fear is absent, our *soul* will express our essential and inherent morality. If we continue in ways that are fearful, prejudiced and condescending toward those who are different, however, we lock ourselves into an us-against-them mentality, engendering hate, retribution, and ultimately war. We need to transcend these rigid and negative impediments of culture, while keeping and developing those qualities that contribute to our adaptive humanity. Our survival on the planet depends on this cultural evolution.

THREE: COUNSELING, CULTURE, AND POLITICAL CORRECTNESS

 ### *Counseling Is Not Value-Free*

Clearly I am not value-free. I am a product of my culture, my generation, my family, my education and other factors noted earlier in this chapter. My dad and my mom were not perfect, but one of the great gifts they gave to me and to my brother Loren was freedom of choice, accompanied by their support and confidence that we would make wise choices. I count their love as the foundation for my positive views of life's opportunities. Here are some of the things I learned to value from my family and larger cultural circle:

> I value freedom
> I value personal responsibility
> I value people who contribute to the greater good
> I value openness and honesty
> I value people who are not defensive and who make themselves
>   open to friendship, and to giving and receiving love

Given all this, the question needs to be asked: How do I monitor my values as a counselor? How do I keep from being Mr. *me!* Optimistic, Mr. Happy or Mr. Apparently Coping Well, in such a way as to make room for my client's explorations and discoveries of his or her own *soul?*

Summarizing a national survey of clinical psychologists, psychiatrists, marriage and family therapists, and clinical social workers, Richards, Rector and Tjeltveit (1999) document that most of these professionals agreed that certain values and healthy lifestyles are used to evaluate and guide therapy. They suggest that most therapists endorsed values such as "personal responsibility, family commitment, self-control, humility, self-sacrifice, forgiveness and honesty." They quote a study by Richards and Bergen which found that "Many therapists continue to implicitly advance their value agendas during treatment..." They go on to identify

> *four problematic therapeutic value styles, all of which tend to impose therapists' values and reduce clients' freedom to make choices about the direction of their lives.*
> - *Deniers believe that by accepting their clients' values, they can avoid imposing their own values*
> - *Implicit Minimizers believe they can minimize their influence by not revealing their own values*
> - *Explicit Imposers believe that their clients will be happier and the world would be a better place if they get clients to accept their values. For example: They contend that their beliefs about certain issues (e.g., gender roles, sexual orientation, religion) are correct.*
> - *Implicit Imposers believe their values are correct but do not openly promote them, only covertly attempting to convert their clients.* (p. 137)

In this book, I am an "explicit imposer." I'm not sure it's possible to impose on readers, since you can always stop reading, but I am certainly suggesting as strongly as I can that my point of view merits consideration. In my work as a therapist, I am at times no doubt guilty of being an "implicit minimizer," or "denier," and probably an "implicit imposer." I am not value-free. While I truly do not want to *impose* my values, I am not against challenging my clients to examine those values of their own which are not serving them well. I am also not opposed to having my values and beliefs known, if my clients are interested enough to choose to read my books, or to attend one of my workshop presentations.

Wing-Sue, Ivey and Peterson (1996), in developing their case for a metatheory of multicultural counseling and therapy (MCT), posit several assumptions and corollaries. In their opening statement of corollary 3D they write:

> *Professional helpers to date have insufficiently considered issues of dominance and power in their helping theories. The very words counselor and client or therapist and patient imply an important hierarchy of power. Historically, much of traditional Western therapy has served a racist, sexist, homophobic and classic culture. MCT recognizes the problems inherent in the power imbalance in current counseling and therapy, and works toward power sharing and mutual construction of therapeutic strategies and goals between therapist and client. Much feminist therapy and culturally sensitive therapy offer this egalitarian approach.* (pp. 17-18)

We know from all the foundational work in multicultural understanding in the past score of years that we must hear and honor the cultural context of our clients. Perry Francis (1998) said it clearly:

> *To ignore someone's spiritual and/or religious background is, in essence, to say in another dimension, "I'm not going to pay attention to the fact that you are Hispanic or African American. I'm not going to take into account those particular issues and how they've affected you."*

Roshni Daya (2000) a counselor educator at the University of Calgary, has, through extensive study of the literature and traditions of Buddhist psychology, identified seven core principles which may be applied across cultures in psychotherapy. In keeping with the Buddha's eight-fold path, I have taken the license to add one more:

"1. Flexibility of self
2. Being in the present
3. Experiencing without evaluation
4. Compassion

5. Openness
6. Interdependency
7. Sitting with suffering"
8. *Awareness*

❖ *Tradition Says "Stay," and Soul Says "Actualize"*

Since our clients' dilemmas are often founded in the collision between culture and their *soul* longing for freedom, we need to keep our values out of the mix in order for them to explore the depths and the roots of their confusion. Our responsibility is to encourage our clients to go deeply into their struggles *without offering advice or answers from our values perspective.* I want to engage my clients to explore their heritage and to understand their own development as it has been impacted by their immediate and extended culture, to see the connections, and to see the consequences.

With regard to training professionals in spirituality, health and multi-cultural differences, Miller and Thoreson (1999) write:

We believe that it is not necessary (or even feasible) for health professionals to be trained in the specifics of the broad array of spiritual and religious perspectives that may be represented among their clients. What a clinician needs, beyond appropriate initial and continuing education, is a set of culturally sensitive proficiencies:

- *A nonjudgmental, accepting and empathic relationship with the client*
- *An openness and willingness to take time to understand the client's spirituality as it may relate to health related issues*
- *Some familiarity with culturally related values, beliefs and practices that are common among client populations likely to be served*
- *Comfort in asking and talking about spiritual issues with clients*
- *A willingness to seek information from appropriate professionals and coordinate care concerning clients' spiritual traditions.*

Sensitivity to the cultural values, mores and points of view of our clients means that we attempt to understand their dilemmas and bring into focus the struggles between the desire of their *souls* to be free and the forces of their culture pulling them to remain loyal to their traditions.

To a great extent, we are all captives of our respective cultures. Some cultural injunctions will impinge particularly harshly on individual freedom and human rights. When our clients' development is impaired and their freedom of choice is limited by their cultural traditions, we must challenge those imposing injunctions in a sensitive and supportive manner.

Pitfalls of Being "Politically Correct"

The problem with being "politically correct" is very much like the problem of being co-dependent. Both states have a tendency to foster behaviors that may be counterproductive to a person's development. As counselors we have been trained to be vigilant and politically correct in all matters of cultural differences. This sensitivity, compassion, understanding and empathy is fine, but we need to make certain that our efforts not to offend the client do not have the outcome of perpetuating his or her neurosis. Our sensitivity to being "politically correct" should not lead us to fall into the trap of over-identifying with a client's culture, such that we fail to challenge her or him to face the dilemmas of the *soul*.

Juan, for example, is Roman Catholic, and the first American-born son of Mexican immigrants. He is married to Anita, of third-generation Protestant Northern European heritage. Juan's cultural model for male behavior in marriage, and with women generally, is to be dominant. Although this behavior becomes a cliché, and may be labeled "machismo" or "macho," there is a certain validity assumed by the frequency of the observed stereotype. Ultimately this cultural trait — learned so well at the feet of his father, grandfather, uncles and other males in his culture — isn't working very well in his marriage to a woman whose peer culture is charging her with feminist injunctions, particularly the part about being equals. Juan is also having trouble at work. The office policy is very clear about gender equality and he has some difficulty taking direction from his immediate supervisor, who happens to be a woman. He is very anxious and extremely fearful that he could lose his job — and his marriage.

As his counselor, it is clear to me that I can't encourage Juan's native cultural inclinations, since they contraindicate movement toward his goal of staying married and staying employed in a changing America. And yet, within the professional culture of counselors, the injunction is to be politically correct, and our tendency has been to bend over backward in honoring the culturally different person. We have been encouraged to show great respect and deference for indigenous traditions. How do we do this when we see that the traditional behavior of the culture is non-egalitarian? How do we remain congruent and honor our own *soul* truths? How do we reveal our values and feelings without casting judgment? These are all delicate questions and issues. In Juan's case, my way would be to challenge his counterproductive behavior with Anita and with his supervisor at work, and to explore with him the consequences of the polarities of his dilemma.

Shun Lee offers another example of a cultural/*soul* collision. This twenty-four-year-old Asian woman faces strong cultural rejection from her parents and extended family because she is dating a Caucasian man ten years her senior. She wants to break free from her cultural restrictions and taboos, but the price of rejection and the threat of loss, and ostracism from her family and larger culture are very costly. As her counselor, I believe it is my job to invite her to get all her fears, hopes, frustrations, guilt, love, confusion and options out and on the table to look at, sort through, and consider, as she ultimately determines *her own* best path. It is her very *soul* that is struggling for autonomous expression, and her choices will have enormous consequences.

❖ *Transcending the Warrior Mentality*

Modern day males are still hunting and gathering (mostly money, sex and other symbols of status), and defending their territory.

But we are evolving, however slowly as we see this territory defined in contests on playing fields. Many men identify with our modern day athletes (surrogate warriors), and with "their" teams, which may be said to represent our primal tribes. One does not have to have extraordinary perception to notice that men have passionate bonds and great loyalty to their chosen teams. Often at social gatherings, the male conversation is dominated by such themes as: who is going to the Super Bowl, the World Series, or the NCAA championships. Bonding to a team stimulates feelings of belonging, and replicates the ancient echoes of tribal memberships. Men may be known more by which teams they identify with than by which political party they support. Sometimes vicarious identification with a sports team becomes argumentative, even obsessive. But for the most part, it is good-natured and creates fellowship among the devoted. Unfortunately, sports talk so often dominates conversations among men that it serves to keep them from relating to each other in more personal and intimate ways.

❖ Snares in the Pursuit of Plumage

The plumage of male birds attracts mates. In the Amazon rain forest, the male of one species of bird kept developing longer and longer tail plumage because the ones with the longest and most colorful tail plumage got to breed the most. Ultimately the plumage got so long, the male birds could not fly! I watched this evolutionary paradox illustrated in a television program years ago, and it occurred to me that as males in our culture, we may be doing the same thing. We can get caught up in the glamour and seduction of life in the fast lane. We, too, may crash or be grounded. In our western affluence, we too often neglect a serious acknowledgment of our *souls*. Our questions are too often focused on our plumage:

- Can I impress someone?
- Can I pass the test?
- Will I be as good as my competitor?
- Can I make enough money?

And finally, in disillusionment, we ask: What do I do with all this stress and pain now that I have impressed someone and passed the test? We can get trapped in our sensual and sexual world, and in our competitive striving.

The great seduction of our capitalistic culture is the plumage of money and status. Our most dangerous trap is greed, because it builds social hierarchies that contaminate our sense of fairness, ever widening the gap between the haves and have-nots. I'm reminded of the biblical question, *What good is it to gain the whole world and lose your soul?*

While women may also get caught up in fashionable plumage, they are generally way ahead of men in their noncompetitive consciousness. There is a long tradition of compassion, sensitivity, openness, and gentleness that serves them well. It is no doubt one of the reasons they live longer than men.

❖ *To Be or Not to Be... Transparent: The Counselor's Dilemma*

I believe it is fair to say that counselors in most western cultures want their clients to be autonomous and to respect human rights. How then do we conduct our work of counseling with respect for our clients who come from cultures which restrict the freedom of women, or which restrict freedoms of speech, assembly and press? In our current state of awareness of and respect for cultural differences, how do we as counselors respond to a couple in counseling when the man insists on traditional values of a paternal society where only the man is the breadwinner, and the male voice is the authority on family matters?

Do we as counselors believe there is a fundamental responsibility to speak out in support of the strengthening of individual freedom of spirit in the life experiences of our client? Can we come down on the side of respect for individual human rights without pushing our agenda or lecturing on morality?

I am clear that as a counselor, I cannot support my clients' loyalty to cultural injunctions which require them to lie, or to keep family secrets which burden them with living a lie, or to allow abusive relationships to continue. I cannot simply "accept" such great costs to the well-being and full-functioning of my client. I want my cultural values to be transparent. I have to be honest with my own *soul*. Clearly I believe that respect for individual differences, for free choice and personal responsibility for decision making support the full development of the human being.

❖ *Diversity: Assimilating the Best*

In spite of archaic weaknesses in human rights in some cultures, every culture on every outpost on the planet has much of value from which we can learn. We need to recognize and honor these ethnic traditions, as the great blending of nations evolves toward the common good of humanity. The integrative weaving of these cultural fabrics will make us stronger, and will ultimately support the individual development of unique cultures as well.

❖ *Soul Searching Journal Assignments — for Your Clients, and for Yourself*

- Reflect on the Shaping Forces of Culture and circle the three that have most affected you. Write a short essay about each.
- Review the list of five culturally sensitive proficiencies developed by Miller and Thoreson (1999), and rate yourself on where you stand. (See page 124.)
- Think about any snares you may have encountered from your culturally defined roles and how you may have been trapped by them.
- Reflect on Daya's List on a Buddhist psychology and write a sentence or two assessing yourself on each.

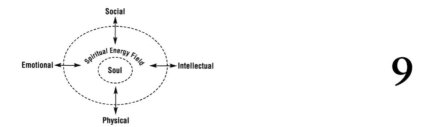

Reflections on "Soul"
Differentiating Spirituality and Religion

Religions through recorded history have been the dominant form of expression of human spirituality. They have named the terms for that which is sacred, composed the rituals, dogmas and hymns, and given material shape to the personal and collective voices of our spiritual life.

Churches and temples have provided the primary places for us to *be* spiritual, to worship, and to acknowledge that which is sacred. They have hosted spiritual ceremonies to honor our marriages, births and deaths in the most sacred way we know how. Religions have given us the form and the context for such traditions, and provided much cohesion to hold us together as a people. Whether it is church on Sunday, temple on Saturday, or bowing in prayer to Mecca several times a day, religions in most cultures continue as our dominant and most defining spiritual force.

As individual beings, the vast majority of us continue to have some need to belong to the larger group, and are drawn to various religions or denominations for their beliefs, rituals, ceremonies and traditions. The need to belong to a family, a tribe, a clan, a community is part of a lifelong biological, social and spiritual structuring of our identity. It is being part of and among the group that we discover and shape the way we define ourselves to others. Clearly we want to be affiliated with a group in which we feel a kinship, a place of being embraced by those we can love and be loved in return.

Abdicating Our Spirituality to the Culture of Religion

In most cultures, religion has been so dominant in defining the personal spiritual life of members that any independent thinking, thoughtful reflection or discussion that diverges from traditional religious doctrines is considered somewhat heretical. And if we as individuals accept this label of *heretical* out of feared consequences, we empower religion, further abdicating our personal responsibility to think for ourselves. If we fail to look within ourselves to claim our spirituality in the face of negative judgment and fear of rejection, we yield to cultural conformity and to ready-made answers that don't invite discussion or individual thinking. Until we take the courage to explore and discover our inner spirituality, and challenge those aspects of dogma with which we may disagree, we are choosing to be captives of pre-ordained traditions.

Many religions have not encouraged the individual and unique personal development of the *soul*. Their emphasis continues to be on their own particular doctrine and their focus toward an external deity. Most religions argue that they stand for an enlightened spirit, one that permits them to feel *worthy, grateful, confident, forgiven* and *self-accepting*. But my experience with many clients and graduate students, and with the culture at large, often tells me the opposite. When there is a strict religious doctrine emphasizing sin, guilt and shame, conforming members are left with a dampened spirit, feeling *unworthy, ashamed, guilty, unforgiven*, and *full of self-doubt and self-judgment*.

In earlier times, harsh injunctions from church doctrines had survival value because of their ability to build cohesion and keep order. As we evolve toward spiritual enlightenment, however, we see these injunctions as anachronistic, bound by time, and severely limited by the defining boundaries of earlier generations.

Many will transcend the culture of their childhoods, challenging the traditions and values that were imposed upon them, including their religious beliefs. They will seek personal meaning and autonomy fulfillment apart from the folks of their origins and the structures of the family's religion.

Leaving Is Not Easy

How do we leave the security of our origins to discover and honor our personal connection with our own *souls*? How do we explore our own most sacred *self* without dishonoring and disconnecting from our families and significant others? How do we access this dimension of our reality? How do we discover that we can be spiritual without being religious? How do we individually find a way to express our gratitude, our reverence, our love for life and all earth's creatures without dogma, doctrine or dictates? How do we find the strength and integrity to stand alone or to find our way as we struggle with moral dilemmas to determine what is right, and what is good? How willing are we to wrestle with these questions as individuals, apart from our group of Methodists, Jews, Catholics, Muslims, Buddhists, or...?

The questions come easily. The answers are a lot more challenging. It's rare to find those who are willing to separate themselves from the norms of the religious traditions of their particular subculture, and come face to face with their own personal spiritual quest.

Transcending Culture and Religion

Breaking with the injunctions of one's religion and culture is not easy. But Carl Jung (1958) gives us one particularly good example of such transcendence. Looking to his father and to the church of which his father was a minister, Jung found nothing but sterility and unacknowledged doubt and confusion. It was then that he ceased to look for God outside himself, determining that if God were to be found, the search had to be inward. It was a turning point, not just for Jung, but — as a result of his writing and speaking — for all of the western world. It was a huge contribution toward a shift in human consciousness. To break with one's culture takes enormous courage and commitment to personal growth. It takes a strong sense of *self* to be a lonely voice, challenging traditions, risking ridicule and rejection. Such strength comes from trusting our *soul* voices, the truth of which we feel and experience in our inner world.

❖ *Can We Separate Spirituality and Religion?*

As behavioral scientists, we are not above the trappings and pressures of cultural norms; indeed, we are immersed in them. As a result, we have avoided taking on this study of the human spirit. We have been cautious and timid in stretching our boundaries of exploration beyond our bonds with religion. Our writing and research continues to couple spirituality and religion, and the linkage between the two is almost always implied, if not stated.

A recent article, "Advances in Conceptualization and Measurement of Religion and Spirituality: Implications for Physical and Mental Health Research" (Hill and Pargament, 2003), trumpets this bond of spirituality with religion one more time. Of over 100 references listed, fewer than ten percent suggested in their titles that they were exploring spirituality as an entity separate from religion. Even among these, most writers paired religion and spirituality in their text. To their credit, Hill and Pargament suggest in their concluding statement that "... there is evidence that religion and spirituality are distinctive dimensions that add unique explanatory power to the prediction of physical and mental health" (p. 72).

Rayburn (2004), goes further: "... unless religiousness and spirituality are separated for research purposes, there will be such a confounding and conundrum effect that understanding of either to any real extent will be seriously prohibited." Later she writes:

> *Furthermore, to propose that there is no spirituality or no mature spirituality outside of religion leads to the* erroneous conclusions *that atheists, agnostics, and individuals not affiliated or identifying with any religious group can never be spiritual and that only theists are to be considered spiritual (caring for others, seeking goodness and truth, transcendence, and forgivness/cooperation/peacefulness).* (Emphasis added).

I believe that religion and spirituality are distinctive, and may be studied apart from each other as well as together. While spirituality is the larger domain, and subsumes religion, our traditions have expressed just the opposite. Religion has dominated the thinking, behavior and writing so totally as to obscure and cast doubt upon alternative avenues of expressing our spirituality. I believe it's time we changed that paradigm.

❖ *The Subculture of the Spiritually Non-Religious*

I would define "the subculture of the spiritually non-religious" as those individuals who have a *personal* sense of their own spirituality and of that which is sacred, apart from any organized religious belief system. These are people who are able to take great meaning from their life experiences, and able to access feelings of reverence, gratitude, humility, respect, compassion and love, without belonging to or believing in any religious orthodoxy. These are people who have a sense of their own *souls* and a connection to a higher power from within, as well as a deep capacity for standing in awe at the mystery of the universe and the beauty of the natural world.

As we let in the wonder of living on a planet that is part of a larger universe, we glimpse still another level of our spiritual essence. Omar Khayyam (1905 and 1914) expresses it beautifully in this piece from the *Rubaiyat* — one of my personal favorites:

> *And that inverted bowl we call the sky*
> *Whereunder, crawling coop't we live and die*
> *Lift not your hands to it for help*
> *For it as impotently moves as you and I.*

Clearly, we must look within for our spiritual essence, seeing our connectedness to the magnificent mystery of all of life, and noticing that this does not require membership in an institution of human design.

There is a large sub-culture of non-religious people who consider themselves to be spiritual but have little or no interest in any organized religion. This would be my group, and I have no idea how many of us there are. It's not that I am adamantly opposed to religion; I'm not. It is just that the dogmas laid down as the price for membership don't seem right for me.

Not to be affiliated with an identifiable religion seems to imply rejection of that which is deemed *holy* by the church. Such persons are often labeled with wastebasket categories *heretic, heathen, pagan, agnostic* and *atheist*. Yet many, many people are drawn to counter-cultures outside of religion, and define their spirituality in various ways that they believe to be no less sacred than the memorized prayers and hymns that glorify an external deity at a specific hour (or hours) on a specific day (or days).

You don't have to be religious to know that love, compassion, caring and other acts of altruism are spiritual in nature, and that they arise within each of us from a much deeper place than logic or compliance to tradition. It is this deeper place of *soul* that is the core of our helping professions.

❖ *Not Demeaning Religion*

I want readers to know that it is not my intention to knock religion. I realize that organized communities of believers continue to serve enormously important functions in our various cultures. I am simply calling for a fair look at the larger spiritual questions, about which those of us without religious affiliations still wonder.

- What is tangible and real about spirituality for me?
- How can I connect with my own sense of the sacred?
- What is the meaning of life for me?
- Who am I in the universe?
- How can I depart from the boundaries that my religious culture has placed on me as requirements for membership, and still be a holy person, a whole person?

❖ *Spirituality in Counseling*

The American Counseling Association helps us to identify how we might integrate spirituality into counseling with the list of competencies developed by one of their divisions, the Association for Spirituality, Ethics, Religion, and Values in Counseling (ASERVIC).

Competencies for Integrating Spirituality into Counseling (ASERVIC, 2004)

Competency 1 — The professional counselor can explain the difference between religion and spirituality, including similarities and differences.

Competency 2 — The professional counselor can describe religious and spiritual beliefs and practices in a cultural context.

Competency 3 — The professional counselor engages in self-exploration of religious and spiritual beliefs in order to increase sensitivity, understanding and acceptance of diverse belief systems.

Competency 4 — The professional counselor can describe her/his religious and/or spiritual belief system and explain various models of religious or spiritual development across the lifespan.

Competency 5 — The professional counselor can demonstrate sensitivity and acceptance of a variety of religious or spiritual expressions in client communication.

Competency 6 — The professional counselor can identify limits of her/his understanding of a client's religious or spiritual expression, and demonstrate appropriate referral skills and generate possible referral sources.

Competency 7 — The professional counselor can assess the relevance of the religious and/or spiritual domains in the client's therapeutic issues.

Competency 8 — The professional counselor is sensitive to and receptive of religious and/or spiritual themes in the counseling process as befits the expressed preference of each client.

Competency 9 — The professional counselor uses a client's religious and /or spiritual beliefs in the pursuit of the client's therapeutic goals as befits the client's expressed preference.

In earlier chapters, I have looked at love and compassion, caring, acceptance, respect, and the myriad *soulful* dimensions between people which affect health and wellness. These spiritual qualities may be seen both within and apart from religion, and they are the key human dimensions of successful counseling relationships that promote healthy relationships and effective living. In light of this, it is very interesting that these qualities have not been addressed as "spiritual" in our graduate training programs or in the preponderance of our professional literature until very recently. We have been too deferential to cause-and-effect science, and too afraid to name and claim our *soul* and spirit.

Our spiritual domain is the source of our vitality! Isn't it time we acknowledge this and get clear about what really goes on between people? While the form, structure and traditions of our religions may help us find meaning and many avenues of expression for that which is sacred, the undeniable reality of the existence of our individual *souls* must be acknowledged, studied and understood as we evolve in our professional world of human service, apart from as well as within the context of our religious experiences.

I believe there are a large number of people who are ready to acknowledge these most vibrant questions of life. Peter Mayer (1999), a songwriter, singer, philosopher, poet, and story teller, speaks to us of these matters in his song "Holy Now."

When I was a boy, each week
On Sunday, we would go to
  church
And pay attention to the priest
He would read the holy word
And consecrate the holy bread
And everyone would kneel
  and bow
Today the only difference is
Everything is holy now
Everything, everything
Everything is holy now.

Read a questioning child's face
And say it's not a testament
That'd be very hard to say
See another new morning come
And say it's not a sacrament
I tell you that it can't be done

This morning, outside I stood
And saw a little red-winged bird
Shining like a burning bush
Singing like a scripture verse
It made me want to bow
  my head

I remember when church let
  out
How things have changed
  since then
Everything is holy now
It used to be a world half there
Heaven's second rate hand
  me down
But I walk it with a reverent air
'Cause everything is holy now.

— Peter Mayer

Soul Searching Exercises — for Your Clients, and for Yourself

- Do you define your personal spirituality within, or apart from, an organized religion?
- Do your own spiritual beliefs reflect those of your parents? Why or why not?
- Do you consider spirituality an appropriate topic to be explored in counseling?

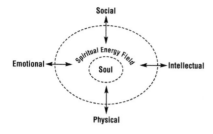

The Emerging Counselor of the New Millennium

All possibilities of human destiny are asleep in your soul.

— John O'Donahue (1997)

The task before us is to awaken our consciousness to a place of honoring our spiritual life as the most meaningful dimension of being fully human. Most professionals know that there is a deeper resonance within us that speaks from the heart. But in our training and functioning as counselors, this *soulful* dimension of the human spirit has been too long submerged.

As our spiritual consciousness rises, we will experience this deeper resonance in all our relationships. We will come forward from behind our social and professional masks and connect person-to-person with greater authenticity. Each of us enters professional service with a unique and diverse belief system and spiritual heritage. As we become more aware of our own spiritual lives, we also become more open to the spiritual differences of others. William Miller (1999) makes a strong case that issues of spiritual diversity should be an integral part of our professional training. In his closing statement, Miller warns us that

> *To overlook or ignore them is to miss an important aspect of human motivation that influences personality development, relationships and mental health... Unlike religion, spirituality*

is part of every individual, an aspect to be understood in gaining a comprehensive picture of a person... one's spirituality, like personality, is complex and multi-dimensional. It encompasses beliefs and motivation, values and meaning, and behavior and subjective experience. (p. 255)

The Ostrich Syndrome

We know full well that within each of us there is an inner wisdom. We just don't talk about it much, or call it what it is. It is astonishing to me that we don't acknowledge this inner spiritual domain somehow in the counseling professions! This is particularly poignant since this inner wisdom is the very dimension that we are trying to empower within our clients! To mix metaphors, it's not just that we are burying our heads in the sand like the ostrich. Our delusion is compounded by being just the opposite of not seeing that the emperor was naked: we don't see *our own* nakedness! We are so laden with the armor and customs of our professional culture, we too often fail to acknowledge the interior landscape of our fellow humans in the very profession that was designed for the study of (ology) the *soul* (psyche).

Awareness Begins with the Self

Before we set ourselves to attending to the spiritual dilemmas in the lives of others, we need to be aware of our own inner life and to become friendly with matters of our own *soul.* When we are clear and centered ourselves, we will live our lives in ways that will demonstrate our readiness to be of assistance to others. The greater our awareness of our possibilities, the greater our menu of choices for developing our total *self.* If we are confident about ourselves as effective choosers and doers, we invite our clients to be the same.

We all have barriers that keep us from exploring our inner life. Our first level of awareness is to see these barriers, and our second is to commit to challenging ourselves to transcend them. Carl Rogers (1980) reminds us that

It is the overstress on the conscious and the rational and the underestimation of the wisdom of our total reacting organism that prevent us from living as unified, whole human beings. (p. 250)

Each of us is on our own spiritual path. But for many of us, the path is blurred by the clutter of life in the fast lane. We get caught up in the mainstream of materialism, neglecting to attend to where we want to go with our lives. If we will but take time to reflect and listen to our inner wisdom, we will seek balance and move toward purpose and meaning in creative ways. To access our inner life requires an ongoing openness to seek the truth about ourselves. My most recent messages tell me to slow down and be open to my compassion in my engagements with others. I want to appreciate all the vitality within relationships more fully. I want to be more open and present for all the possibilities that exist in each day. Frances Vaughn (1986) triggers these thoughts in me when she writes,

Every decision chooses the future. You are free to choose the qualities that you want to express in the world, just as you are free to choose the beliefs and attitudes that you accept into your mind.

If I am to evolve toward wisdom, it is truly up to me to wake-up and to act.

I was inspired (infused with spirit) by Carl Rogers (1980), when he wrote of the "Qualities of the Person of Tomorrow." I've taken the liberty of borrowing from his list and adding my own.

Qualities of the Person of Tomorrow
(after Rogers, 1980)

WE ARE TRANSCENDING

FROM AN EMPHASIS ON	TOWARD AN EMPHASIS ON
rigid roles & appearance	authentic behavior
hierarchical dominance	egalitarian relationships
secrecy	openness

(cont'd,)

prejudice and exclusion	respect and inclusion
individual effort	collaborative effort
competition	cooperation
knowing by rote memory	knowing how to find out
from deference to authority	autonomy and internal authority
exploiting nature	ecological reverence
national identity	global consciousness

❖ *Spiritual Qualities of the Counselor*

We are waking up and coming to see that our *spiritual energy* is manifest in every thought, attitude, belief and action. Certainly any act of love, any expression of gratitude, reverence and respect stems from the quality of our spiritual life. In this same vein, Brian Thorne (1998) writes: "I must live as if I have vast resources for loving and need to find channels for that loving." (p. 122)

Here are some other qualities toward which our consciousness is evolving.

- An inner peace and the ability to express love.
- A sense of meaning and purpose, which is rooted in serving to make our world a better place.
- An inner knowing that our best self and highest wisdom is found within our own life force, which seeks health and balance.

When we are open to our inner world, we access more imagination, more intuition and spontaneity, and we become more responsive.

Emerging Training Emphasis

It is a travesty that our graduate programs in the helping professions have been more interested in the applicant's grade point average and scores on the Graduate Record Exam than they have been in the personal qualities of the candidate's human spirit. To be sure, knowledge is an important foundation for being an effective helper of others. But it requires much more of the person wishing to be a helper than an advanced degree in areas of specialized knowledge. Before knowledge can be usefully assimilated, counselors must be willing to enter into rigorous self-examination of their own *souls*. Whether we are counselors, psychologists, psychiatrists, social workers, therapists, educators or others in the helping professions, we need to understand our own motives and intentions, our own values and priorities.

Among the more salient outcomes of such *soul* searching are these:

- A high level of self-awareness of our own spiritual burdens, fears, hostilities and anxieties, with a willingness to explore the source of these and how to transcend them.
- An openness and flexibility to learn how others see us, with the ability to let go of any patterns of prejudice or inclination to be judgmental, and not to have our own issues triggered inappropriately by our clients.
- A willingness to become...
  ... centered and stable
  ... able to love freely with genuine caring & respect
  ... capable of interacting warmly and confidently
  ... more authentic and fully present in the moment.

I believe the education of counselors and others who will do the work of human service must be drawn from the ideas and ideals that concern themselves with the essence of the human spirit. We need to recognize and address our spiritual domain in all human relationships. In this regard, Brian Thorne (1998) pays a high compliment to those who train counselors:

> *Not infrequently now, I find myself viewing counseling sources in higher education as monasteries of a new dark age, for they keep alive the vision of a world where persons matter more than things and where mutuality and understanding are more important than achievement and competition.*

He goes on about these issues in professional training:

Having come clean about this primacy of love in the therapeutic enterprise I do not wish to be accused of naiveté or sentimentalism. Love, as I mean it in this context, clearly demands the most rigorous training and levels of self-knowledge and self-acceptance that are unlikely to be attained without effort except by the most fortunate and beloved of persons (p. 54).

To access such a place of love and optimism, we must challenge our long-standing traditions of conceptualizing people's difficulties in negative terms, such as depression, distress and anxiety. While these labels may be helpful in framing the person's overall tone, the emphasis and focus of treatment should be toward that which is possible. Dunn (1961), one of the early thinkers and writers in the human potential movement, defined wellness as "an integrated method of functioning which is oriented toward maximizing the potential of which the individual is capable" (p. 4).

❖ I Owe My Soul to the Company Store: Institutions, Agencies, Private Practice

What does it mean then to think of ourselves as *soul* counselors when we may think that the company store holds the mortgage on our *soul*?

"Yes Dwight, it's nice that you want us to be autonomous and recognize that we have *souls*, and that our deepest and most meaningful connections are at the *soul* level with others, but it may not be safe to talk about these things at work."

I understand that your livelihood and your loyalties may be tied up with your workplace, which has policies and standards of practice that may seem to rule out *soul* as a focus of your practice. Each workplace is a culture unto itself, and we know that it is important to fit in if we are to feel supported and create growth conditions for ourselves. Some institutions and agencies will be open and flexible, giving us room to be our unique selves, while others will require strict adherence to policies, curbing more intuitive individual expression. Even in conservative workplaces, I believe it is a matter of personal willingness to frame your own beliefs in *soulful* terms. It is a matter of emphasis in what we value in our daily contact with clients. Some may fear judgmental consequences and keep a low profile about their personal spiritual matters, wondering, "Would my colleagues, supervisors, friends still love me if they knew I was a *soul* counselor?"

While I'm being somewhat facetious here, I want to make the point that I think many, if not most, people at this time in our culture may be a little hesitant to claim a *spiritual* or *soul* focus as the primary fibers of connection between people. I think it takes courage to stand up for your own spiritual beliefs. It's not a black-and-white issue and need not be adversarial. You can be a loyal professional within traditional settings and still work within the cultural language structures, while paying close attention to what is going on with the *soul* of your client.

For example, if you are working in a college counseling agency, and a sophomore presents as struggling with her parents' impending divorce, her uncertainty about what she should major in, and whether she should just avoid dating for now until she figures everything out, these are three very major existential dilemmas that are impacting her *soul*. She is not just cognitively concerned, or emotionally upset. Her emotions will be in turmoil; she will be cognitively, socially, behaviorally and sexually confused. And she'll be trying to assimilate and integrate the meaning of events so she can determine her best course of action. Are these not *soul* issues?

Similarly, if you are a career counselor, and your client announces that he has wasted his time for the past twenty years in a job and career path that was going nowhere, it is a much deeper issue than simply trying to help him find a rewarding job or a career. He is looking for meaning, purpose and satisfaction, all three of which are *spiritual* quests (the last of which is also a very desirable state of being).

Frances Vaughn (1986) speaks to the heart of this matter for counselors:

> ... *a healing relationship can be any one that favors the development of awareness, self-esteem, trust, growth, freedom,*

well-being, and transcendence. A healing relationship makes it safe to let go of masks and defenses, and allows one to be fully present in a free-feeling exchange with another person (p. 186)

It doesn't matter if you are working in private practice, community agencies, hospitals, clinics, or schools, the challenge to recognize and work within this spiritual domain is imperative if we are to truly acknowledge the whole person we call our client or patient. Recognizing the *soul* and *spiritual energy* of our clients will take our work to new and more meaningful levels.

Elaine, a former client, brought herself for counseling declaring that her marriage was over! She simply would no longer put up with her husband Jim's bullying, and his attempts to control her with his anger. It was very clear that her spirit was rising. She stood up for herself to face her husband, the challenges in her marriage, and the consequences of her emerging autonomy. My recognizing this strength within her gave her confidence as she continued to stand up to her verbally abusive and controlling husband. After just a few weeks, Jim got Elaine's message quite clearly, as he faced the prospective consequences of the dissolution of his marriage and family. His attitude and demeanor softened, dropping some of his self-righteous armor, agreeing to a more egalitarian relationship.

I believe that when a person brings him or herself for counseling, something is trying to happen within that person. Just acknowledging this nebulous "something" helps the client to clarify and define just what it is that wants to come forward and grow. It is also extremely important to acknowledge the movement your clients make toward growth. It validates them in a way that they may not be able to validate themselves because of self-esteem issues and the tendency to be self-effacing. As Elaine felt validated, she actually made a transformational shift from a culture of abuse, where she was a passive victim, toward a culture where she would develop as a more assertive and autonomous woman. The overall outcome has been a very strong positive expression of her *soul.*

In his later years, Carl Rogers (1980) was more able to integrate his spiritual nature into his writing about what was going on within him during a therapeutic encounter. He wrote:

I find that when I am closest to my inner, intuitive self, when I am somehow in touch with the unknown within me, when perhaps I am in a slightly altered state of consciousness, then whatever I do seems to be full of healing. Then, simply my presence is releasing and helpful to the other. There is nothing I can do to force this experience, but when I can relax and be close to the transcendental core of me, then I may behave in strange and impulsive ways in the relationship, ways which I cannot justify rationally, which have nothing to do with my thought processes. (p. 129).

Burke and Miranti (1995) echo Rogers' notion of a transcendent core, writing that:

Counselors must be prepared to deal with all issues, including the quality that lies at the very core and essence of the client's being. That core, which transcends the physical and material aspects of existence, which is untouchable and oftentimes indefinable, is so necessary for an explanation to one's existence. Clients themselves often suggest that spirituality is the sustaining core or essence that keeps them going when all else seems to fail. (p. 2)

They go on to say:

... neglecting to draw on the spiritual values that clients hold may deprive them of a singular sense of strength and support in times of great need. This is particularly true as persons grow older and they seem to exhibit a greater desire to explore religious/spiritual issues. These clients need counselors who are not afraid to address their spiritual needs and who are comfortable with their own spiritual selves... the challenge is not whether the issue of spirituality should be addressed, but how it can best be addressed by well-prepared and sensitive professionals. (p. 3)

Only in recent history have we begun to see ourselves and our survival as linked to the well-being of all people, and indeed to all life forms. This vision has not been an easy passage, nor will it be totally resolved in our near future, but we are working on it. The good news is, there is a great spiritual awakening and our continuing commitment to this rising of human consciousness emerges from the stirrings of the individual *souls* of each of us.

The importance of this individual awareness is captured in the following poem attributed to Vaclav Havel, president of the Czech Republic:

BEGINNING TO BE

It is I who must begin...
Once I begin, once I try,
here and now,
right where I am,
not excusing myself
by saying that things
would be easier elsewhere,
without grand speeches and
ostentatious gestures,
but all the more persistently
– to live in harmony
with the "voice of Being," as I
understand it within myself
– as soon as I begin that,
I suddenly discover,
to my surprise, that
I am neither the only one,
nor the first,
nor the most important one
to have set out
upon that road...
Whether all is really lost
or not depends entirely on
whether or not I am lost...

— Václav Havel

Heroes to Emulate

It is not our sports or war heroes who will move us toward spiritual evolution, it is the greatness of those who seek justice. It is Abraham Lincoln, Mohandas Gandhi and Martin Luther King. It is Nelson Mandela and Vaclav Havel. It is all those who have evolved to a consciousness of living together harmoniously on the planet. Until we all arrive at this consciousness, there will be no complete justice, no true peace.

Schools as Centers for Human Development

To educate a person in mind and not in morals is to educate a menace to society.

— Theodore Roosevelt

We must start early in education if we are going to sow the seeds for transformation and create the kind of world we want. We need to make it our *priority* to pass on to our children the best of what is known about being fully human. In our human service professions, we need to honor the depth, breadth and centrality of our spiritual life, the essence which drives our humanness. We should make certain that these most significant of encounters are taught as our highest values and passed on with more than haphazard or random lessons.

Brian Thorne (1998) again reminds us,

Raising standards, improving the quality of teaching, providing evidence of achievement — they all sound like worthy objectives and they appeal to those who relish hitting targets and obtaining hard data. But many teachers know — even those who find it difficult to express themselves with adequate feeling — that learning depends ultimately on love, love between teachers and taught, and love for the subjects that are being studied. (p. 106)

Clearly we must not lose sight of the human element, the *soul* connection a great teacher makes with her students. It is education that will create the opportunity for continuing the evolution of our awareness. It will be education that teaches tolerance, teaches respect, teaches love and teaches that all life is sacred. We need to accelerate our movement toward this more wholistic consciousness if we are to learn to live together peacefully.

In a personal conversation I had in 1979 with renowned psychiatrist William Glasser, he said "Before we can feel worthwhile we must act worthwhile." This resonated with great truth for me at the time, and while it is true that acting worthwhile will bring us the rewards of recognition and make us feel worthwhile, I believe there is a piece missing here. I would say now, that *before we can feel worthwhile we need to be cared about and respected in our infancy and early childhood. This foundation of love will give us the strength and character to act in a worthwhile manner.* And so it follows that:

- Before we can express love we must experience being loved, being cared about, valued, and prized.
- We must experience encouragement before we can give encouragement to others.
- We must feel accepted before we can accept others.

Only in the last forty or fifty years are we beginning to develop these spiritual qualities in our schools, and it is interesting that we do not honor the richness of our spiritual life to anywhere near the extent that we honor achievement in athletics, technology, money gathering, sexual attractiveness, being cool or entertaining. Why not acknowledge and celebrate acts of kindness, love, generosity and respect? Why not systematically create tangible examples of these experiences in our schools, and call them *spiritual*, because they are? It is important to claim the depth and breadth of these most human of behaviors, and teach our children to appreciate the spiritual qualities that are within themselves, and in all people of every age, color and shape. We can do more to foster human development. Kindness, fair play, cooperation, trust and tenderness are all experienced with abundant tangible examples. More and more, we see the implementation of structured learning activities designed to develop a multitude of spiritual human traits throughout the life span. We need to continue expanding these curricula from their beginning foundations. Consider these *soul* areas that could be further developed in education:

- Wellness over the life span
- Nutrition
- Physical fitness
- Relationships and sexual intimacy
- Marriage and commitment
- Balancing work with leisure and recreation
- Issues of meaning and purpose in life

While many of these themes are currently being taught and integrated into some school curricula, this foothold needs to become a priority, and more fully accepted. As members of the professions whose concern is for all humans to develop their full potential, we need to take the courage to advocate these human development agendas because they are a priority. Our survival favors the higher consciousness of cooperation, respect, support, forgiveness, acceptance and love, and these can all be taught.

We can do more with parent education and family interventions. We can do more to reduce the greed and narcissism so prevalent in our culture. We can do more to reduce teasing and bullying, and more to increase respect and compassion for individual differences. Our emerging identity has everything to do with the circumstances we create.

Peter Guerra (1998) acknowledges that character education is making a comeback. He cites the twelve universal values on which the Character Education Institute bases their work:

- Honor
- Courage
- Convictions
- Honesty
- Truthfulness
- Generosity
- Kindness
- Helpfulness
- Justice
- Respect
- Freedom
- Equality

All these issues can be woven into the fabric of our lessons, our interactions, and into specific curricula to develop character in our students throughout the twelve or thirteen years that we have them in schools. Schools are the only social agency in our culture where we have the opportunity for ongoing preventative and developmental programs. A school is the only institution for the common good through which every child will pass. The younger the child is when we intervene, the better the outcome. Character education *is* spiritual development.

Jeff Kottler (2000), in his book *Doing Good*, writes:

> *There would seem to be certain people who hold a strong sense of equity and generosity, almost as a part of their personalities. In reviewing the research to date on so-called altruistic personalities, especially among children who show early signs of doing good for others, Hunt (1990) found that the following characteristics were most often in evidence:*
>
> 1. *Happy, well-adjusted, popular kids were more likely to be helpful to others than those who are sad, isolated, or in bad moods.*
> 2. *Young children who are emotionally expressive and sensitive are more likely to respond to others in trouble.*
> 3. *High self-esteem was associated with helpful acts, since people are more inclined to extend themselves to others who they perceive as worse off than they are. (pp. 26-27)*

These qualities, developed in children, will be with them for a lifetime. Clearly this is the kind of world we want to build.

There has been much important work that has been done to lay the foundation for the emerging person of the new millennium. Our challenge now is to create a climate in our culture that will bring *soul* consciousness into the mainstream, and create conditions for every client, every student, indeed, every person to discover and claim their spiritual strengths.

I close with a piece from *The Prophet*, by Kahlil Gibran (1982), who reminds us that all work is empty save when there is love, and that work is love made visible.

> *And what is it to work with love?*
> *It is to weave the cloth with threads drawn from*
> *your heart,*
> *even as your beloved were to wear the cloth*
> *It is to build a house with affection,*
> *even as your beloved were to dwell in the house*
> *It is to sow the seeds with tenderness and reap the*
> *harvest with joy, even as if your beloved were to eat*
> *the fruit*
> *It is to charge all things you fashion with a breath*
> *of your own spirit.*

Soul Searching Journal Assignments — for Your Clients, and for Yourself

- Rate yourself (from one to five with five as highest rating) on the *Qualities of the Person of Tomorrow* (pp.143-144). Comment on what you need to do for growth.
- Write about how your work in human services contributes to meaning and purpose in your own life.
- Write about your inner peace and your ability to express and receive love.
- Write about what you think we could do to bring about more spiritual awareness in our work in human services. How might you contribute to this effort?
- What barriers are you aware of that keep you from exploring your inner life?

APPENDIX

Counseling Forms and Agreements

My Counseling Perspective

Client Autobiographical Reflections

Client Self-Perspective

*Client Autobiographical, Cultural,
and Relationship Considerations*

Client Significant Events

*Client-Counselor Agreements
of Understanding*

My Counseling Perspective
— Dwight Webb, Ph.D. —

I see healing as emerging from within our human spirit, and it is the vitality
of your spirit that I want to engage, and to challenge you to empower
yourself. I will respond not so much to the details as to the meaning of
what you share. My job is not to judge but to try and understand, and
to help you to discover your own path. I will share my thoughts, feelings,
opinions, values and ideas as they relate to our work together, when I think
it will be helpful. My personal philosophy is one of hope and optimism.

Soul counseling is a journey exploring your joys and sorrows, the
high and low points of your everyday experiences, as well as your deepest
longings and dreams. I invite you to share these in our work together
knowing that they will be honored. Your growth on this journey will
depend very much on your willingness to open your heart to all that is
you, as we work together. I work from a wholistic perspective that may
be seen in the model below.

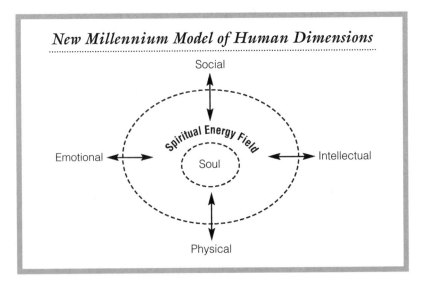

Client Autobiographical Reflections

Take some time to reflect on your experiences, and your thoughts, and feelings. Write your responses in your journal and bring these to our next session.

- Social Relationships

- Intellectual Interests and Pursuits

- Emotional Balance

- Physical Condition

- Spiritual Beliefs

Here are some questions to ask yourself

- Can I be real and open with others?

- How easy or difficult is it for me to let love into my life?

- How easy or difficult is it for me to express my love to others?

- Old patterns of behavior that no longer serve me well?

- What are my core values?

- What are the things that are most important to me?

- What gives my life meaning?

- If I could fulfill my life, I would...

(Use back side if necessary)

Client Self-Perspective

Evaluate yourself from a 1 (low) to a 5 (high).

I am secure and confident in social situations   _____

I am happy and cheerful with others   _____

I am friendly, warm and caring   _____

I see myself as a peaceful and tranquil person   _____

I take initiative in reaching out to make contact
with others   _____

I have a good balance between independence,
interdependence   _____

I am willing to be open with others   _____

I am a respectful and moral person   _____

I am responsible and trustworthy   _____

I am dependable, and people can count on me   _____

I am comfortable with intimacy   _____

I have the ability to love deeply   _____

(In your journal, write down anything you may want to expand upon)

Here are some other personal spiritual qualities to consider

	Needs Work	Doing Well	Comments (use back side)
COMPASSION			
GENEROSITY			
GRATITUDE			
KINDNESS			
COMMUNICATION			

Client Autobiographical, Cultural, and Relationship Considerations

Our families, communities and larger culture all have great bearing on who we are: our attitudes; our choices and behaviors; our perceptions; our beliefs.

The following will help you to identify those people and experiences that have had a significant impact on your life. Write about how and why in your journal:

- Your father

- Your mother

- Any siblings (list by age and gender)

- Your significant peers

- Other people (teachers, coaches, aunts, uncles, etc.) who were significant

- Your educational experiences

- Your work experiences

- Your community and sense of your socio/economic status

- Any discrimination you may have experienced

- Thoughts on your sexual development

- What gives your life meaning and purpose?

- Any traumas in your life in any way?

(Use back side if necessary)

Client Significant Events

CHILDHOOD
AGE.............................EVENT   Negative 1-5   Positive 1-5

TEEN YEARS
AGE.............................EVENT   Negative 1-5   Positive 1-5

ADULTHOOD
AGE.............................EVENT   Negative 1-5   Positive 1-5

CURRENT
AGE.............................EVENT   Negative 1-5   Positive 1-5

(Use back side if necessary)

Client-Counselor Agreements of Understanding

As a client, I agree to

1. Bring no harm to myself or to others;

2. Put concerted effort into my own personal growth during the 167 hours of each week between sessions. This would include cooperating with assignments such as behavioral rehearsals, understanding cognitive distortions, bibliotherapy, etc.;

3. Be challenged toward my growth path;

4. Explore my own resistance;

5. Write my personal reflections in my journal on a regular basis.

Signature of Client _____

As your counselor I agree to:

1. Serve as a guide and facilitator of your growth process within a trusting and safe environment;

2. Share my observations and give you feedback of my impressions;

3. Have faith in and believe in you;

4. Work for your well-being and healthy functioning in every way;

5. Maintain professional and ethical standards throughout our work.

Signature of Counselor _____

Bibliography

Alexander, C. N., & Langer, E. (1990). *Higher stages of human development.* New York: Oxford University Press.

Allenbaugh, K. (2000). *Chocolate for a woman's blessings.* New York: Fireside/Simon & Schuster.

Anglund, J. W. (2001). Opening quotation in chapter five in K. Allenbaugh. *Chocolate for a woman's blessings.* New York: Fireside.

Arterburn, S., & Furton, J. (1991). *Toxic faith: Understanding & overcoming religious addiction.* Nashville, TN: Oliver Nelson.

Arthur, N. (1998). Counsellor education for diversity: Where do we go from here? *Canadian Journal of Counselling 32*: 88-103.

Assagioli, R. (1965). *Psychosynthesis: A manual of principles and techniques.* New York: Viking Penguin.

Assagioli, R. (1989). Self-realization and psychological disturbances. In S. Grof & C. Grof (Eds.), *Spiritual emergency: When personal transformation becomes a crisis* (pp. 27-48). Los Angeles: Jeremy P. Tarcher.

Association for Spiritual, Ethical, and Religious Values in Counseling. (2004). *Guidelines for Integrating Spirituality into Counseling.* Alexandria, VA: ASERVIC.

Auel, J. (1980). *The clan of the cave bear.* New York: Crown.

Banks, R. (1980). Health and the spiritual dimension: Relationships and implications for professional preparation. *The Journal of School Health, 50,* 195-202.

Banks, R., Poehler, D., Russell R. (1984). Spirit and human-spiritual interaction as a factor in health and health education. *Health Education,* 16-19.

Barnhouse, R. T. (1979). Spiritual direction and psychotherapy. *Journal of Pastoral Care, 33(3),* 149-160.

Barret, R. L. (1988). The spiritual journey: Explorations and implications for counselors. *Journal of Humanistic Education and Development, 26,* 155-162.

Bart, M. (1998 December) Spirituality in Counseling: Finding Believers. *Counseling today.*

Bemak, F., & Epp. L. (1996). The 12th curative factor: Love as an agent of healing in group psychotherapy. *Journal for Specialists in Group Work, 21(2),* 118-127.

Bensley, R. (1991 November/December). Spiritual health as a component of worksite health promotion/wellness programming: A review of the literature. *Journal of Health Education, 22(6).*

Benner, D. G. (1991). *Counseling as a spiritual process.* Oxford, UK: Clinical Theology Association.

Bergin, A. E. (1988). Three contributions of a spiritual perspective to psychotherapy and behavior change. In W. Miller & J. Martin (eds.), *Behavior therapy and religion: Integrating spiritual and behavioral approaches to change* (pp. 25-36). Newbury Park, CA: Sage.

Bergin, A. E., & Payne, I. R. (1991). Proposed agenda for a spiritual strategy in personality and psychotherapy. *Journal of Psychology and Christianity, 10,* 197-210.

Berthold, S. M. (1989). Spiritism as a form of psychotherapy: Implications for social work practice. *Social Casework, 3,* 502-509.

Boadella, D. (1998 March). Essence and ground: Towards the understanding of spirituality in psychotherapy. *International Journal of Psychotherapy.*

Booth, L. (1995). A new understanding of spirituality. In R. J. Kus (Ed), *Spirituality and chemical dependency* (pp. 9-17). New York: Haworth.

Bowman, R. L. & Baylen, D. (1994). Buddhism and second-order change. *International Journal for the Advancement of Counselling 17:* 101-108.

Brehony, K. A. (1999). *Ordinary grace: An examination of the roots of compassion, altruism, and empathy, and the ordinary individuals who help others in extraordinary ways.* New York: Riverhead Books.

Brown, G. I. (1979). (author of *Confluent Education,* among others). Comments on Gestalt techniques. Guest alumnus presentation in a seminar for the faculty at the University of New Hampshire Department of Education.

Buber, M. (1970). *I and thou* (W. Kaufmann, translator). New York: Scribner.

Burke, M. J. & Miranti, J. G. (1995). *Counseling: The spiritual dimension.* Washington D.C., American Counseling Association.

Bynum, E. B. (1994). *Transcending psychoneurotic disturbances: New approaches in psychospirituality and personality development.* New York: Haworth Press.

Campbell, J. (1988). *The power of myth.* New York: Doubleday.

Campbell, J. (1990). *The transformations of myth through time.* New York: Harper & Row.

Capra, F. (1982). *The turning point.* New York: Simon and Schuster.

Carlson, W., & Shield, B. eds. (1989). *Healers on healing.* Los Angeles: Jeremy P. Tarcher.

Chandler, C. K., & Kolander, C. (1992). Counseling for spiritual wellness: Theory & practice. *Journal of Counseling & Development. 71(2),* 168-175.

Chandler, C. K., & Kolander, C. A. (1988). Stop the negative, accentuate the positive. *Journal of School Health, 58(7):* 295-297.

Chappel, J. N. (1990). Spirituality is not necessarily religion: A commentary on "Divine Intervention and the Treatment of Chemical Dependency." *Journal of Substance Abuse, 2,* 481-483.

Chapman, L. (1987, Fall). Developing a useful perspective on spiritual health: Love, joy, peace and fulfillment. *American Journal of Health Promotion, 1*, 31-39.

Chapman, L. (1987 Fall). Developing a useful perspective on spiritual health: Well-being, spiritual potential and the search for meaning. *American Journal of Health Promotion (2).*

Chopra, D. (1989). *Quantum healing.* New York: Bantam Books.

Claxton, G. (1986). The light's on but there's nobody home: The psychology of no-self. In G. Claxton (ed.). *Beyond therapy: The impact of eastern religions on psychological theory and practice* (pp. 49-70). London: Wisdom Publications.

Clinebell, H. (1995). *Counseling for spiritually empowered wholeness.* Binghamton, New York: Haworth Press.

Coles, R. (1990). *The spiritual life of children.* Boston, MA: Houghton Mifflin.

Cortright, B. (1997). *Psychotherapy and spirit: Theory and practice in transpersonal psychotherapy.* Albany, New York: State University of New York Press.

Cousineau, P. (Ed.). (1990). *The hero's journey: Joseph Campbell on his life and work.* San Francisco: Harper.

Cousins, N. (1981). *Human Options.* New York: Berkely Books.

Cousins, N. (1983). *Head first: The biology of hope and the healing power of the human spirit.* New York: Avon Books.

Daya, R. (2000). *Buddhist psychology, a theory of change process: Implications for counseling* (22: pp. 257-271). Netherlands: Klener Publications.

Deikman, A. (1982). *The observing self: Mysticism and psychotherapy.* Boston: Beacon Press.

Dickinson, E. (1951). "If I can stop one heart from breaking." The Belknap Press of Harvard University Press.

Doherty, W. J. (1995). *Soul searching.* New York: Basic Books.

Donnelly, D. (1993). *Spiritual fitness: Every day exercises for body and soul.* New York: Harper Collins.

Dossey, L. (1993). *Healing words.* San Francisco: Harper-Collins.

Dossey, L. (1989). *Recovering the soul.* New York: Bantam Books

Dyer, W. (1989). *You'll see it when you believe it.* New York: William Morrow and Company.

Dyer, W. (1995). *Your sacred self.* New York: Harper Collins.

Elgin, D. (1980). The tao of personal and social transformation. In R. Walsh, F. Vaughan (Eds.) *Beyond Ego: Transpersonal dimension in psychology.* (p. 253). Los Angeles: Jeremy P. Tarcher.

Elkins, D., Hedstrom, L., Hughes. L., Leaf, J., Saunders, C. (1988). Toward a humanistic phenomenological spirituality. *Journal of Humanistic Psychology, 28,* 5-18.

Ellison, C. W. (1983). Spiritual well being: Conceptualization and measurement. *Journal of Psychology and Theology, 11(4)*, 330-340.

Epstein, M. (1995). *Thoughts without a thinker*. New York: HarperCollins Publishers.

Ferrucci, P. (1982). *What we may be: Techniques for psychological and spiritual growth through psychosynthesis*. Los Angeles: Jeremy P. Tarcher.

Ferguson, M. (1980). *The aquarian conspiracy: Personal and social transformation in the 1980's*. Los Angeles: Jeremy P. Tarcher.

Fisher, C. (2001). Psychological assessment: From objectification back to the life of the world (Issue II) in Slife, B., Williams, R., And Barlon, S. (eds.) *Critical issues in psychotherapy: Translating new ideas into practice*. Newbury Park, CA: Sage.

Fowler, J. (1981). *Stages of faith: The psychology of human development and the quest for meaning*. San Francisco: Harper and Row.

Fox, R. (2003, August). Address to the Annual Convention, American Psychological Association, Toronto, Ontario.

Francis, P. (1988 December). As quoted by Mary Bart, *Counseling Today*. Washington: American Counseling Association.

Frankl, V. E. (1959). *Man's search for meaning*. New York: Washington Square Press.

Frankl, V. E. (1957). *The doctor and the soul: An introduction to logotherapy*. New York: Alfred Knopf.

Frankl, V. E. (1958). The will to meaning. *Journal of Pastoral Care, 12*, 82-88.

Fromm, E. (1956). *The art of loving*. New York: Harper and Row.

Frost, N. H., Ruge, K. C. & Shoup, R. W. (2000). *Soul Mapping: An imaginative way to self-discovery*. New York; Marlowe & Co.

Fukuyama, M., & Sevig, T. (1997). Spiritual issues in counseling: A new course. *Counselor Education and Supervision, 36*, 224-232.

Fukuyama, M., & Sevig, T. (1999). *Integrating spirituality into multicultural counseling*. London: Sage.

Gawain, S. (1978). *Creative visualization*. New York: Bantam Books.

Gawain, S. (1986). *Living in the light*. Mill Valley, CA: Whatever Publishing.

Gawain, S. (1988). *Reflections in the light: Daily thoughts and affirmations*. San Rafael, CA: New World.

Georgia, R. T. (1994). Preparing to counsel clients of different religious backgrounds: A phenomenological approach. *Journal of Counseling and Values, 38*, 143-151.

Gladding, S. (1999). The faceless nature of racism: A counselor's journey. *Journal of Humanistic Education and Development, 37(3)*, 182-187.

Gladding, S. T. (2004, September). Diagnoses, labels, dialogue. *Counseling Today*.

Gibran, K. (1951). *The prophet*. New York: Alfred A. Knopf.

Glantz, K., & Pearce, J. K. (1989). *Exiles from Eden: Psychotherapy from an evolutionary perspective*. New York: Norton.

Glasser, W. (Author of *Reality Therapy* and other books. Named a "Living Legend in Counseling" by the American Counseling Association in 2004. Personal communication).

Goleman, D., Smith, H., Dass, R. (1985). Truth and transformation in psychological and spiritual paths. *The Journal of Transpersonal Psychology, 17*, 183-215.

Gordon, T. (1970). *Parent effectiveness training*. New York: Wyden Press.

Gorsuch, R. & Miller, W. (1999). Assessing spirituality. In Miller, W. (ed.) *Integrating spirituality into treatment* (chapter three). Washington: American Psychological Association.

Grof, S. (1988). *Adventure of self-discovery: Dimensions of consciousness and new perspectives in psychotherapy and inner exploration*. AlbaNew York: State University of New York

Guenther, H. V. & Kawamurea, L. S. (1975). *Mind in Buddhist psychology*. Emeryville, CA: Dharma Publishing.

Guerra, P. (1998, October). Universal values and character education. *Counseling today*.

Havel, V. (1983). It is I who must begin. From *Letters to Olga* (Paul Wilson, translator). New York: Henry Holt and Co., Inc

Hendricks, G., & Weinhold, B. (1982). *Transpersonal approaches to counseling and psychotherapy*. Denver: Love Publishing.

Hesse, H. (1951). *Siddartha*. New York: New Directions.

Ho, D. Y. F. (1995). Selfhood and identity in Confucianism, Taoism, Buddhism, and Hinduism: Contrasts with the west. *Journal for the Theory of Social Behaviour 25(2)*: 113-139.

Horney, K. (1956). The search for glory. In C. E. Moustakas (Ed.), *The self* (pp.39-51). New York: Harper & Row.

Hubble, M. A., Duncan, B. L., & Miller, S. D (1999). *Heart and soul of change*. Washington: American Psychological Association.

Hunt, M. (1990). *The compassionate beast: What science is discovering about the humane side of humankind*. New York: William Morrow.

Iannone, R. V. & Obenauf, P. A. (1999). Toward spirituality in curriculum and teaching. *Education* (Summer).

Ingersoll, R. E. (1994). Spirituality, religion and counseling: Dimensions and relationships. *Journal of Counseling and Values, 38*, 98-111.

Jaffe, D. T. (1980). *Healing from within*. New York: Bantam.

Jennings, L., & Skovholt, T. M. (1999). The cognitive, emotional, and relational characteristics of master therapists. *Journal of Counseling Psychology, 46(1)*, 3-11.

Jones, S. S. (1987). *Choose to be healthy*. Berkeley, CA: Celestial Arts.

Jourard, S. (1964). *The transparent self: Self-disclosure and well-being*. New York: Van Nostrand.

Joy, Susan. (1973,1978,2004). *All kinds of weather friends*. Amherst, NH: BMI (Boston Post Rd.)

Jung, C. (1958). *The undiscovered self*. (RFG Hall Translation). New York: Mentor Books.

Jung, C. G. (1933a). *Modern man in search of a soul*. New York, New York: Brace and World-Harvest.

Kasl, C. D. (1992). *Many roads, one journey: Moving beyond the twelve steps*. New York: Harper Perennial.

Kelly, E. W. (1995). *Spirituality and religion in counseling and psychotherapy: Diversity in theory and practice*. Alexandria, VA: American Counseling Association.

Kessler, R. (2000). *The soul of education*. Alexandria, VA: Association for Supervision and Curriculum Development.

Khayyam, O. (1905 and 1914). *The Rubaiyat of Omar Khayyam*. (The Fitzgerald translation). New York: Dodge Publishing Co.

Kornfield, J. (1993). *A path with heart*. New York: Bantam Books.

Kottler, J. (2000). *Doing good: Passion and commitment for helping others*. Philadelphia: Brunner Rutledge.

Krishnamurti J. (1953). *Education and the Significance of Life*. New York: Harper and Row.

Kurtz, E. (1999). The historical context. In Miller, W. (ed.) *Integrating spirituality into treatment: Resources for practitioners* (chapter two). Washington: American Psychological Association.

Lapsley, J. N. (1993). Spirit and self. *Pastoral psychology, 38(3)*, 135-146.

Larsen, E., & Hegart, C. (1991). *Believing in myself*. New York: Bantam.

Laszlo, V. S. (Ed.) (1054). *The basic writings of C. G. Jung*. New York: Random House.

Locke, S. & Colligan, D. (1986). *The healer within*. New York: Mentor.

Loomans, D. (1999, Spring). If I had my child to raise over again. *Parent Partners Newsletter*. Davidson, NC: Exceptional Children's Assistance Center.

Maltz, M.(1969). *Psycho-cybernetics*. New York: Pocket Books

Maslow, A. H (1970). *Motivation and personality*. New York: Harper & Row.

Maslow, A. H. (1971). *The farther reaches of human nature*. New York: Viking.

Maslow, A. H. (1968). *Toward a psychology of being* (2nd ed.). NewYork: Harper & Row.

Maslow, A. H. (1980). A theory of metamotivation: The biological rooting of the value-life. In R. N. Walsh & F. Vaughn (Eds.), *Beyond ego: Transpersonal dimensions in psychology*. Los Angeles: Jeremy P. Tarcher.

May, G. G. (1988). *Addiction and grace: Love and spirituality in the healing of addictions.* San Francisco: Harper & Row.

May, G. G. (1982). *Care of mind, care of spirit: Psychiatric dimensions of spiritual direction.* San Francisco: Harper & Row.

May, R. (1991). *The cry for myth.* New York, New York: Norton.

Mayer, Peter. (2001). "Holy Now." From his album, *Million Mile Mind.* Available by email at *peppermint@actwin.com*

Mearns, D. and Thorne, B. (1999). *Person-centered counseling in action* (2nd ed.). London, UK: Sage Publications.

Miller, G. (1999). The development of the spiritual focus in counseling and counselor education. *Journal of Counseling & Development, 77,* 498-501.

Miller, W. R. (ed.) (1999a). *Integrating spirituality into treatment: Resources for practitioners.* Washington: American Psychological Association.

Miller, W. R. (1999b). Diversity training in spiritual and religious issues (chapter seven, p. 255). In William R. Miller (ed.), *Integrating spirituality into treatment: Resources for practitioners.* Washington: American Psychological Association.

Miller, W. R. and Thoresen, C. E. (1999). Spirituality and health. In William R. Miller (ed.), *Integrating spirituality into treatment: Resources for practitioners.* Washington: American Psychological Association.

Moberg, D. O. (1971). *Spiritual well being: Background.* Washington: White House Conference on Aging.

Moody, H. R. & Carroll, D. (1998). *The five stages of the soul.* London: Random House.

Moore, T. (1992). *Care for the soul.* New York: HarperCollins.

Moore, T. (1994). *Soul mates: Honoring the mysteries of love and relationship.* New York: Harper-Collins.

Moss, D. (ed.) (1999). *Humanistic and transpersonal psychology.* Westport, CT: Greenwood Press.

Myers, J. E. (1990, May). Wellness throughout the lifespan. *Guidepost* (p. 11).

Naisbitt, J. (1982). *Megatrends: Ten new directions transforming our lives.* New York: Warner Books.

O'Donahue, J. (1997). *Anam Cara: Spiritual wisdom from the celtic world.* New York: Bantam.

Oliner, P. M., & Oliner, S. P. (1995). *Toward a caring society: Ideas into action.* Westport, CT: Praeger.

Ornish, D. (1998). *Love and survival: The scientific basis for the healing power of intimacy.* (Chapter Two). New York: HarperCollins.

Ornstein, R. & Sobel, D. (1989). *Healthy pleasures.* Reading, MA: Addison-Wesley

Ornstein, R. & Sobel, D. (1987). *The healing brain.* New York: Addison-Wesley

Parry, S. J. & Jones, R. G. A. (1986). Beyond illusion in the psychotherapeutic enterprise. In G. Claxton (ed.), *Beyond Therapy: The impact of eastern religions on psychological theory and practice* (pp. 173-192). London, UK: Wisdom Publications.

Peale, N. V. (1987). *The power of positive thinking* (new condensed edition). Pawling, NY: Center for Positive Thinking.

Peck, M. S. (1978). *The road less traveled: A new psychology of love, traditional values and spiritual growth*. New York: Touchstone.

Peck, M. S. (1995). *In search of stones: A pilgrimage of faith, reason and discovery*. New York: Hyperion.

Pennebaker, J. W. (1990). *Opening up: The healing power of confiding in others*. New York: William Morrow.

Perls, F. (1969). *Gestalt therapy verbatim*. Layfayette, CA: Real People Press.

Ram Dass. (1989). Promises and pitfalls of the spiritual path. In S. Grof & C. Grof (Eds.) *Spiritual emergency: When personal transformation becomes a crisis* (pp. 171-187). Los Angeles: Jeremy P. Tarcher.

Ram Dass, & Bush, M. (1992). *Compassion in action*. New York: Bell Tower.

Ram Dass, & Gorman, P. (1985). *How can I help? Stories and reflections on service*. New York: Knopf.

Richards, P. S. & Bergin, A. E. (1997). *A spiritual strategy for counseling and psychotherapy*. Washington: American Psychological Association.

Richards, P. S., Rector, J. and Tjeltveit, R. (1999). Values, spirituality and psychotherapy. In W. R. Miller (ed) *Integrating spirituality into treatment* (chapter seven). Washington: American Psychological Association.

Rogers, C. (1961). *On becoming a person*. Boston, MA: Houghton-Mifflin.

Rogers, C. (1977). *Carl Rogers on personal power: Inner strength and its revolutionary impact*. (p. 3). New York: Delta.

Rogers, C. (1980). *A way of being*. Boston, MA: Houghton-Mifflin.

Rosenthal, P. and Jacobson, L. (1968). *Pygmalion in the classroom*. New York: Holt Rinehart and Winston.

Salinger, T. E. (1969). *The spiritual needs of the aging: In need of a specific ministry*. New York: Alfred A. Knopf.

Sarason, S. (1995). *Caring and compassion in clinical practice*. Northvale, NJ: Jason Aronson.

Schaef, A. W. (1999). *Living in process: Basic truths for living the path of the soul*. New York: Ballantine Wellspring.

Schneider, L. A (1998, December). In M. Bart. Spirituality in counseling: Finding believers. *Counseling today*.

Seaward, B. L. (1991). Spiritual well-being: A health education model. *Journal of Health Education, 22(3)*, 166-169.

Seligman, M. (1992). *Learned optimism*. New York: Pocket Books.

Sheldrake, P. (1992). *Spirituality and history: Questions of interpretation and method*. New York: Crossroad.

Siegel, B. S. (1986). *Love, medicine and miracles*. New York: Harper & Row.

Sivananda Companion to Yoga, The. (2000). New York: Simon and Shuster.

Small, J. (1982). *Personal transformation: The way through*. Marina del Rey, CA: DeVorss.

Smith, H. (1991). *The world's religions*. San Francisco: Harper.

Smith, M. L. (1989). *The word is very near you*. Cambridge: Cowley.

Smith, M. L .(1991). *A season for the spirit*. Cambridge: Cowley.

Smith, S. G. (1988). *The concept of the spiritual: An essay in first philosophy*. Philadelphia: Temple University Press.

Sober, E., & Wilson, D. S. (1998). *Unto others: The evolution and psychology of unselfish behavior*. Cambridge, MA: Harvard University Press.

Spengler, O. (1926). *The decline of the west*. New York: Alfred Knopf.

Spitz, R., & Cobliner, G. (1965). *The first year of life*. Madison, CT: International Universities Press.

Stuart, E., Deckro, J., Mandle, C. (1989). Spirituality in health and healing: A clinical program. *Holistic Nursing Practice, 3*, 35-46.

Tart, C. T. (1990). Adapting eastern spiritual teachings to western culture. *Journal of Transpersonal Psychology, 22(2)*, 149-166.

Thorne, B. (1998). *Person-centered counseling and Christian spirituality: The secular and the holy*. London, UK: Whurr Publishers.

Tiger, L. (1979). *Optimism: The biology of hope*. New York: Simon & Schuster.

Tillich, P. (1952). *The courage to be*. New Haven, CT: Yale University Press.

Travis, J. & Ryan, R. (1980). *The wellness workbook*. San Rafael, CA: Ten Speed Press.

Truax, C., & Carkhuff, R. (1967). *Toward effective counseling and psychotherapy*. Chicago, IL: Aldine.

Unknown. In Felleman H. (1955). *Poems that Live Forever*. Garden City, NY: Doubleday.

Van Fleet, J. (1994). *The power within*. Englewood Cliffs, NJ: Prentice Hall.

Vaughan, F. E. (1986). *The inward arc: Healing and wholeness in psychotherapy and spirituality*. Berkeley, CA: Shambhala.

Vaughan, F. E. (1991). Spiritual issues in psychotherapy. *Journal of Transpersonal psychology, 23*, 105-119.

Vaughan, F. E. (1979). *Awakening intuition*. New York: Anchor.

Walsh, R. (1999). *Essential spirituality: Exercises from the world's religions to cultivate kindness, love, joy, peace, vision, wisdom, and generosity*. New York: Wiley.

Watts, A. W. (1961). *Psychotherapy east and west*. New York: Vintage Books.

Watts, A. W. (1963). *The two hands of God: The myths of polarity*. New York: George Braziller.

Watts, A. W. (1964). *Beyond theology: The art of godsmanship*. New York: Vintage.

Watts, A. W. (1966). *The book: On the taboo against knowing who you are*. New York: Vintage.

Watts, A. W. (1971). *In my own way*. New York: Vintage.

Webb, D. (1995). Unpublished paper on claiming our spirituality, presented to the Personal Counselling Institute, Dublin, Ireland.

Webb, D. (1999). *50 Ways to Love Your Leaver*. Atascadero, CA: Impact Publishers.

Weil, A. (1990). *Natural health, natural medicine*. Boston, MA: Houghton-Mifflin.

Weinhold, B. (Author of several books including *Transpersonal Counseling*, and more recently a curriculum entitled "The kindness campaign. " This is a program for implementing interpersonal awareness skills. He can be reached at *weinholds@pcisys.net*)

Welwood, J. (2000). The practice of love. *Shambhala Sun* (p. 30).

West, W. (2000). *Psychotherapy and spirituality: Crossing the line between therapy and religion*. London, UK: Sage Publications.

Wilber, K. (1980). A developmental model of consciousness. In R. N. Walsh & F. Vaughan (Eds.), *Beyond ego: Transpersonal dimensions in psychology* (pp. 99-114). Los Angeles: Jeremy P. Tarcher.

Wing-Sue, D. W., Ivey, A., and Peterson, P. (1996). *A theory of multicultural counseling and therapy*. Pacific Grove, CA: Brooks Cole.

Witmer, J. M. (1985). *Pathways to personal growth*. Muncie, IN: Accelerated Development.

Witmer, J. M. and Sweeney, T. (1992, November/December). A holistic model for wellness and prevention over the lifespan. *Journal of Counseling & Development*. Vol. 71.

World Health Organization (1958). Constitution of the W. H. O. annex 1: *In the first ten years of the W.H.O.* Geneva, Switzerland: W.H.O.

Yalom, I. D. (1980). *Existential psychotherapy*. New York: Basic Books.

Yellowbird, M. (2000). Spirituality in first nations storytelling: A Sahnish-Hidatsa approach to narrative. In S. Abels (ed.), *Spirituality in Social Work Practice* (Chapter Nine). Denver: Love Publications.

Index

More Books with IMPACT